RUTILIO GRANDE

Memory and Legacy of a Jesuit Martyr

Ana María Pineda, R.S.M.

lectio
Lectio Publishing, LLC
Hobe Sound, Florida, USA

www.lectiopublishing.com

© 2021 Ana María Pineda, R.S.M. All rights reserved. No part of this book may be reproduced or transmitted in any form or by any means, electronic or mechanical, including photocopying or recording, or by any information storage and retrieval system without prior written permission of the publisher.

Cover image: "Saints of El Salvador" Painting © Peter Bridgman. Used with permission.

Photos inside this book:
© Archivo fotográfico, Centro Monseñor Romero, Universidad Centroamericana "José Simeón Cañas" (UCA), San Salvador, El Salvador. Used with permission.

Cover and Book Design: Linda Wolf

Paperback ISBN 978-1-943901-20-3
Library of Congress Control Number: 2021953548
e-Book ISBN 978-1-943901-22-7

22 January 2022, the Beatification Ceremony of the Salvadoran Martyrs, including Father Rutilio Grande.

Published by Lectio Publishing, LLC
Hobe Sound, Florida 33455
www.lectiopublishing.com

DEDICATION

To my brothers and sisters, nieces and nephews.

For the storytellers, artists and musicians of El Salvador who keep the memory of our Martyrs alive.

ACKNOWLEDGEMENTS

Writing this book is the culmination of a long journey. It began decades ago when I was introduced to the iconic figures of Archbishop Romero and Jesuit Rutilio Grande of El Salvador and began to explore their significance. My initial investigations led to the publication of *Romero and Grande: Companions on the Journey*. Subsequently, I concentrated on the lesser known figure of Father Rutilio Grande, S.J., first martyr of El Salvador and a significant figure not only in the life of Archbishop Romero but in the Church of El Salvador. The result is this modest book that weaves together diverse aspects of Grande's life and ministry. As always, it has been a labor of love made possible with the support of countless friends, colleagues, community members and extended family.

I hold with great affection and gratitude the memory of Monseñor Ricardo Urioste, Rev. Virgilio Elizondo, Robert Pelton, C.S.C., and Brennan Hill who from the beginning, encouraged me in this endeavor and have now joined the Communion of Saints. I also owe a tremendous debt of gratitude to Salvador Carranza, S.J., Rodolfo Cardenal, S.J., Andreu Oliva, S.J., of the Central American University (UCA) in San Salvador, El Salvador, whose support has assisted me in my ongoing research into the life and legacy of Rutilio Grande, S.J. In this effort, Julian Filochowski of The Archbishop Romero Trust has consistently offered me his expertise.

As the title indicates, this book focuses on the collected memory of Father Rutilio. And I am profoundly grateful to the countless men and women whom I have had the privilege to interview over many years and who have lovingly and generously shared their personal recollections of Father Grande. I am indebted to the generosity of Peter Bridgman for his permission to use his artwork for the cover of the book and to Patti Kantor for her generous editing.

As always, I am grateful for the sisterly affection and support of my community of the Institute of the Sisters of Mercy, particularly Sister Carmen Rodriguez and Sister Mary Ann Clifford. I am deeply blessed to be supported by the love of my brothers, Tony, Ernie, Roberto, and sisters Tita, Vilma and their spouses and children. It is my deepest desire that the legacy of our Pineda Escamilla and Grande Pineda family be a source of pride and inspiration not only for our present generation, but also for those to come.

My deep gratitude extends to Santa Clara University for not only facilitating but also encouraging my ongoing work to bring to light the gift we have received from these Salvadoran Martyrs.

Finally, the ongoing contributions to the development and crafting of my writing has consistently been enriched by the sharing of ideas and editorial suggestions of Lourdes Thuesen; she has been a faithful friend and writing companion in this project and many others. Lastly, there are no words to fully express my gratitude to Eric Wolf, my kind editor, not only for his belief in this project but for his determination to publish this book so that the world may come to know and appreciate the profound significance of Father Rutilio Grande, S.J.

FOREWORD

In an age characterized by a steep decline in religious affiliation across denominations, especially among youth and young adults, it may seem unexpected to suggest that the People of God in the recent past were still quite capable of producing men and women of heroic holiness. A careful reading of Sister Ana María Pineda's concise and carefully researched study of Salvadoran martyr and hero Rutilio Grande suggests that saintliness was still to be found in the context of the revolutionary unrest that gripped much of Central America during the decades of the 1970s and '80s. *Rutilio Grande: Memory and Legacy of a Jesuit Martyr* makes a much needed and timely contribution to our knowledge and appreciation of the historical and human context of the brief yet impactful life of Grande and the meaning of his sacrifice.

The hosts of martyrs produced in the second half of the twentieth century in Latin America and in other parts of the Global South provide rich sources of inspiration and wisdom about what is worth living and dying for. Rutilio Grande and his companions, Manuel Solórzano and Nelson Rutilio Lemus, are just three of the scores of committed church workers who have witnessed in our times to the integral connection between Christian faith and justice. Their struggles for justice were enacted in the context of the ordinary ministry of the church and not as a form of political militancy. Their motivation was rooted simply in the love of God and neighbor, not in political calculations flowing from some ideology. Grande opted as a Jesuit to follow Christ in a dangerous world journeying in the footsteps of Christ just as Saint Ignatius of Loyola, founder of the Jesuits, had done centuries earlier. Ignatius framed his experience of God in the Spiritual Exercises where the most repeated words are, "Love shows itself more in action that in words."

Pineda's exploration of Grande's memory and legacy highlights the origins and growth of this man's calling from his *campesino* roots, educational opportunities, vocation to the priesthood and consecrated life, personal struggles, family relations and friendships over a brief forty-nine years of an unassuming and "ordinary" life. Quotations from his letters, homilies and newspaper publications carefully selected by Pineda expose the strong, robust underpinnings of his motivations and convictions. They reveal a man actively in search of integrity who struggles and brilliantly succeeds in discovering who he is and for what or for whom he lives.

A significant take-away from this engaging book pertains to the role of the Second Vatican Council and the response of the Church in Latin America to the social, economic and political context of that continent's marginalized people. Grande's life exemplifies how the Second Vatican Council's option for the poor and oppressed as boldly promoted in its *Decree on the Church in the Modern World (Gaudium et spes)*. Grande's life also witnesses to the impact of basic ecclesial communities as promoted by the Latin American Bishops at their seminal Medellín Conference of 1968. These sources grounded Grande's way of life and profoundly influenced his activities as pastor, writer and teacher as chronicled by Pineda. It was his unflinching fidelity to the renewal and reform of the Church in his own place and time and among his own people that undoubtedly led to his assassination. Pineda makes a fine contribution to our understanding of the people and events that contextualize the development of Grande's heroic participation in the drama of his times.

The work before you exudes a simple elegance in terms of methodology and judicious use of sources. The author's writing is crisp and a gripping story emerges flawlessly pieced together from the available documentation. Of particular interest will be the nuanced treatment given to the relationship between St. Óscar Romero and Grande whom Romero followed to martyrdom just three years later.

Foreword

Finally, the reader of this moving narrative gains a vivid picture of a spirituality of lo cotidiano, everyday life, forged in Grande's habit of daily prayer. The habit was nurtured by his family's and people's faith as well as by his formation in a biblically-rooted Ignatian spirituality. Humility and prayerful attentiveness reveal themselves in Grande's spiritual maturity manifested in his large and little struggles of daily life to which he characteristically responded with love, purposefulness and discernment rather than with raw instinct or mindless routine as so often is the case. In the luminous figure of Blessed Rutilio Grande, beautifully sketched in the following chapters, meet the generous man who faced these experiences and tumultuous events in all their terror and gore. He was tested, but by the grace of God, he was not found wanting.

Allan Figueroa Deck, SJ
Loyola Marymount University

CONTENTS

Dedication

Acknowledgements

Foreword

INTRODUCTION 1

CHAPTER 1 5
Writings
- On Blessing of Schools 6
- On a Marketplace Eviction 8
- On the God of the Military 9
- Christmas for Rural Communities 10
- Priestly Anniversary of Archbishop Chávez y González 11
- Soledad (Our Lady of Solitude) 13
- Published sermons 15
- Perspective 25

CHAPTER 2 31
The Press
- Realidad social Salvadoreña 34
- Violencia sangrienta y Violencia Institucionalizada 35
- Perspective 36

CHAPTER 3 39
Rutilio's Correspondence
- Archbishop Chávez y González 39
- Rutilio Grande and his Health 44
- Letters on Ministry 46
- Grande's Communication with Political Figures 55

Tensions in the Country 58
Family Correspondence 60
Perspective 66

CHAPTER 4 73
Romero's Sermons on Rutilio Grande
Perspective 87

CHAPTER 5 93
Memory and Legacy
Rutilio Grande, the Man 93
Formation of Seminarians 98
A New Model of Church 102
Religiosity of the People 105
Memory Celebrated in Song and Murals 108

APPENDIX 119
March 1977 Photographs

INTRODUCTION

With my family roots in El Salvador, I have always had a special relationship with that small beautiful Central American country and its people. I was born there. My father came to the United States first with the plan to earn a degree in accounting and a dream of returning to El Salvador to make a life for us. When I was two, my mother migrated to the United States with me and my older brother. On arrival, we settled in the Spanish-speaking neighborhood of San Francisco, California affectionately referred to as the "Mission District." In time, my sister and two brothers were added to the family, and my father's dream was put on hold as he worked to provide for our growing family.

In our home, my parents shared stories with us of their childhood and of their hometowns. The names San José Guayabal and El Paisnal became familiar ones, as my mother and father often talked about their families and memories of growing up in El Salvador. Hearing their stories was one of my favorite experiences. Their sharing of memories kept the family story alive. Being inquisitive, I often asked questions about my grandparents, my aunts and uncles. I imagined what they were like, and what it must have been like to grow up in my parents' hometowns. Finally, when I was seventeen, I traveled with my mother to visit El Salvador for the first time. It would be the first of many trips which gave me opportunities to visit my parents' hometowns and to meet family members. During one of my trips to El Salvador visiting my father's family I first heard the name of Rutilio Grande. My uncle Flavio Grande Garcia talked about his younger brother Rutilio as he showed me photos of him. He even encouraged me to travel to Aguilares and visit with his brother Rutilio who was the pastor there. Despite my interest and best efforts, I was not able to meet him. A year later, our family received word that Father Rutilio had been murdered. I was left with the memory of my conversation with my Uncle Flavio, and the photo image of a man with a gentle smile.

Many years have gone by since I first heard of Father Rutilio Grande. Following one shared memory to another, I was on a search to know more about his life, and the circumstances surrounding his assassination. A lover of stories from my childhood years, I began to search out persons who might have known Grande and who would be willing to share their memories with me. In this search, I had the privilege to hear stories about him from the Grande Pineda family, former seminarians that he taught, Jesuit confreres, laity from the parish in Aguilares and from men and women who met him. But beyond the memories shared by people of Father Rutilio, I found myself poring through archival material left behind by Father Grande upon his death. In doing so, I was privileged to meet him through his correspondence, homilies, and published newspaper articles.

In time, I discovered how the story of his life was an integral part of Salvadoran history. Certainly, the people of his hometown of El Paisnal still remembered him as a child growing up in their midst along with his five brothers. They were acquainted with his parents, Salvador Grande and Cristina Garcia. They remembered the struggles young Rutilio and his brothers lived through when their parents separated. They accompanied him from afar as he entered the seminary of San José de la Montaña in San Salvador, and eventually prepared for ordination as a Jesuit. And, years later they took pride in seeing him be named pastor of Our Lord of Mercies in the town of Aguilares a few miles from his beloved hometown of El Paisnal. They witnessed his commitment to the poor, and saw how his preaching of the gospel imbued women and men with confidence and an understanding that God did not want men and women to be poor or to suffer its consequences. Ultimately, his work among the poor presented a threat to those in power. On 12 March 1977 as Father Tilo traveled to St. Joseph Church in El Paisnal, he was shot and killed

Introduction

along with two of his parishioners—72-year-old Manuel Solórzano and fifteen-year-old Nelson Rutilio Lemus. As the country mourned the death of this beloved martyred priest, his body and that of his two companions were taken and buried at the foot of the altar in the parish church of St. Joseph in El Paisnal.

Since his death, the memories of his life has become part of the collective memory of El Salvador. He continues to live in the memories of the people who knew him, in the writings that Grande penned, in the sermons that he preached, in the hymns and murals painted on neighborhood walls throughout El Salvador. This small book gathers them all to offer the reader a glimpse into the life of Blessed Rutilio Grande—martyr and faithful son of the Church and El Salvador. His memory and legacy live on.

CHAPTER 1

WRITINGS
HOMILIES, PASTORAL LETTER, AND OTHERS

Those who knew Rutilio Grande, tragically murdered at the young age of 49, knew him as a gifted and talented communicator. Those who heard him preach and deliver speeches at a variety of gatherings were impacted not only by the content and relevance of his message, but also by his delivery. Few of his many sermons were published but some were recorded by his Jesuit friend and Aguilares team member, Salvador Carranza. After Grande's murder, when the military occupied the town of Aguilares,[1] these recordings, too, were lost. Consequently, there is no extensive record of his sermons, and to date, only three of them have been published.

As Grande actively engaged in the civic life of the country, he was acquainted with the editors of local newspapers. He wrote articles for the *Prensa Gráfica* and *El Mundo* on a number of topics addressing pastoral concerns and shedding light on the realities of the times through the lens of the Gospel.

Drafts and fragments of some of his sermons, copies of a "pastoral letter," a poetic reflection to Our Lady of Solitude, and several newspaper articles were left in his personal files. Fortunately, these were rescued before the military invasion and destruction of the parish belongings in Aguilares where he served as pastor. Although a small collection, these documents provide an insight into Grande's beliefs and the motivation underlying his commitment.

The approximately ten or so drafts of his sermons from his personal files address diverse audiences for a variety of events. Among the sermons are: The "Blessing of a School" (Bendición de Escuela), the Eviction from the Market Stalls (without a title in Spanish), God of the Military (Dios de los Militares), Christmas (Navidad), Te Deum, Homage to Archbishop Chávez y González and the Festival of the Corn (Tercer Festival de Maíz). Woven throughout these writings are themes of Rutilio Grande's deep conviction of what it meant to be Christian in the world of actual reality.

On Blessing of Schools

On at least two occasions, Father Rutilio was invited to speak at the blessing and inauguration of newly constructed school buildings. One new school was in his hometown of El Paisnal and at its opening (26 July 1975), he expressed his gratitude for all that the public event signified:

> I come to bless a work for the good of the community…Hopefully, each day a school will be opened in the country and a bar closed; hopefully, each day a brothel will be closed and a new school opened in the most remote corner of our land… A school is a blessing for the entire community because of all it symbolizes.[2]

Above all, Grande pointed out that this new school symbolized what the country urgently needed in their decisive moment of history, a history of rapid, necessary, and urgent transformations. Education was needed for even the humblest member of Salvadoran society. In Grande's opinion, aside from teaching and transmitting knowledge of science and culture, schools were required to cultivate critical consciousness of the country's realities. It was not sufficient to grasp information offered through encyclopedias or the dictionary, but the mind of each student should be able to personally and creatively respond to the challenges that society presented. Grande emphasized the need for education for the children of the poorest of the poor with the hope that it would prepare future generations who would be conscious of their calling to be agents in forging their own history.

While he attributed his understanding of politics to his study of Greek philosophy including Plato, he was clear on his role as a religious leader. Notably in this sermon at the new school, he reiterated his deep conviction that he was a religious leader and did not belong to any political party,³ an assertion that recurs throughout his sermons and public communications. As he concluded, Grande signaled an important truth:

> The church and its authorities bless and praise all efforts that are made for the common good of the people...regardless of where these achievements or efforts come from. Because as I have said and I repeat, the Church is the bearer of the purest values of the Gospel that coincide with the deepest human aspirations...⁴

On a similar occasion, the dynamic of benediction served as the focal point when he was asked to bless another new school.

> The word blessing is derived from the Latin word *'benedicere'* which means "to say or desire good" about people and things...the desire for health, prosperity, good harvest, success in business, in short, for everything that is good for men and women ... Each transformation of the earth and all that it contains is a blessing from God which is generous and all embracing.⁵

He turns the blessing into a litany of all that benefits humankind... the good highway, and the wide road... a factory that benefits all equally... the land cultivated and transformed with fertilizer, for the good of all and not of a few... a plentiful and rich harvest for all the children of God... a place at the table for all ... the blessing of family brought together in love. When any of these blessings is absent, human beings are unfulfilled. God is absent. Goodness is absent.

> There is no joint effort of men, there is the ambition of some and evil in many. The supreme curse is the sin that festers in the heart of man and corrupts entire groups and communities ...⁶

Finally, Grande extolled the significance of water and why it is used in rituals of blessing. Water transforms arid plains to a land of plenty. Water is used in baptism. In blessing the new school; water is a symbol of the hopes and prayers of the community for their children. Father Rutilio concluded his benediction with the hope that the school would be...

> preparing new generations of peasants, aware of their vocation as free men in the midst of the national community ... We ask God that this school shine like a light in the middle of the community, and that the children who begin their studies, may thereafter continue them, in any area of study, even until arriving at the university classrooms, to which all able Salvadorians must have access, including the humble children of our peasants.[7]

On a Marketplace Eviction

One October Sunday, Father Grande delivered a passionate sermon on a recent banning of the townspeople from their market stalls.[8] Several weeks earlier the Municipal Council had issued an order to evict the local tradespeople from their marketplace posts. In the draft of that sermon, Grande shared his observations and the process that he had followed prior to deciding to speak on the issue. He purposefully gave himself time to reflect, consult and pray over the incident. He re-examined the Constitution of the Republic to see whether there was a political reason that supported the eviction but found none. After his weighing of the Council's action, he found no legitimate reason for the eviction. In light of the outcomes of his personal investigation and reflection, Grande denounced the action of the Municipal Council:

> Therefore, finding no serious and valid motive for such expulsions from the market, we believe that it is unjust, that it is a grave and scandalous sin that we cannot conceal, shut up or cover up, because if we did, we would be complicit in that public (social) sin and we cannot do that in good conscience ... We denounce this injustice as something that goes against the most basic human rights, and naturally against the Gospel that we as baptized have to live and live fully.[9]

In this sermon, true to Grande's theological understanding, a Christian's stance in the world as a baptized member of the

Church required attention to one's civic duties and to the Gospel. Both demands were legitimate and Rutilio understood his priestly obligation as attending to the needs of the entire community regardless of political or religious affiliation. Throughout his life, he consistently reiterated this understanding of his vocation and call. Toward the end of this brief but significant sermon, Father Rutilio reemphasized: "If I have spoken of this fact it is because I must defend all who are trampled over unjustly, whether they be a Protestant brother or someone without religion."[10]

On the God of the Military

Every year on the 7th of May, the people of El Salvador celebrate "Soldiers' Day" to commemorate the founding of its armed forces in 1824. The day is a public holiday celebrated with parades presented by the members of the Armed Forces. For one such day in his parish, Father Grande wrote a brief reflection on the significance of the holiday dedicated to the military. In his commentary he took the opportunity to deliver a deeper message. He pointed out that festivities being held in Aguilares were in the very city that bears the name of Nicolás Aguilar, Vicente Aguilar, and Manuel Aguilar—priests and brothers who worked to liberate the people of El Salvador from the dominion of the Spanish rule. Furthermore, that celebration of Soldiers' Day was being held in their very own city, which was under the protection of Our Lord of Mercies, patron of both the city and parish. Grande connects these historical and religious realities by linking the festivities to the popular practice of the "serenade." As a person is serenaded on the day of his/her birth, so too the faithful serenade Our Lord of Mercies during the civic observation.

> We heard a serenade this morning, in front of the parish temple in honor of the Lord of the Mercies. I hope that we hear the serenade that the Lord of Mercies wants us to hear, all those who claim to be leaders in this country: the serenade of his Gospel, which proclaims the values of justice, brotherhood, love, a new order, to forge a new world ... and to "wake up" to an urgent and

9

necessary change. We have to wake up with that serenade.[11]

Fr. Rutilio's words admonished his listeners to keep in mind their duty to be at the service of the people and not demand to be served by the people.[12] Neither priests nor the military should allow themselves to be bought by a handful of people to the detriment of the community. In his concluding words, Father Grande reminded the military that many of them come from the surrounding communities and often were taken in forced recruitment raids.[13] The members of the military, he contended, belong to the Salvadoran peoples, and they should strive to protect and defend the lives of their countrymen and women. In essence, respect and service toward the people is the authentic way to celebrate Soldiers' Day and to reverence the Lord of Mercies.

Christmas for Rural Communities

Rutilio Grande worked and ministered in rural communities. This was especially true during the years of his pastoral leadership in the parish of Our Lord of Mercies in the large town of Aguilares. Most likely his interest in the rural poor stemmed from his own childhood experience. He was born in the small hamlet of El Paisnal, and suffered the many deprivations faced by poor campesinos.[14] His family struggled to provide for their needs, but there were many days when Rutilio along with his family had little to eat. In spite of the many difficulties, Grande always loved his hometown and had a special affection for the campesinos. Early on in his ministerial interests and studies, he sought to find creative and effective ways to bring the Gospel alive within the daily realities of the rural communities. Gradually, Rutilio gained a reputation as a leading innovator in ministering to the campesino communities. His passion for the campesino is reflected in a very short sermon entitled "Christmas for the Rural Communities" (*Navidad Campesina*) that he delivered on 21 December 1975.

Grande began his sermon by asking the congregation to consider the question: "Yesterday as today, men seek out Jesus and ask—Are you the one that is to come or should we wait for another?"[15]

He reminded his listeners that the answer to that age-old question is Jesus who comes into the world and gives sight to the blind, makes the lame walk, the deaf hear, raises the dead to life. Those signs testify that the kingdom of God is present. And, what did that message reveal to each of those who were listening to Rutilio's sermons? The truth of Jesus' birth is realized in the fact that the Gospel had opened their eyes. Once blind, now they are able to see the reality of injustice and oppression. To become aware of the realities that the people live, the first step is to recognize injustice. Grande continued with an evocative litany of the many signs that reveal that Jesus has come into the world,

> Jesus, his Gospel, has opened our eyes. Before we were blind, now we see our reality of injustice and oppression. Before we were deaf, now we hear the word of God. Before we were silent, now we speak, we defend ourselves, we question, we do not remain silent before the injustice. These are the signs we find in our communities. We desire and seek to remove oppression, injustice in ourselves and in our communities, in our society. These are the signs that Jesus is born in us.[16]

Lastly in addressing the people gathered in the parish church celebrating Eucharist he raised the question: who exactly are the poor? "Those among us," he told them, "without hope, without dignity, without any possibilities of any kind within this society."[17]

He reminded them, however, that the gift given to each is the fact that Jesus brings a new hope on Christmas. Only two things are required. First, that they have faith in Jesus' word and believe that the injustice that torments their lives can and needs to be changed. Secondly, that Christians must unite and organize in the work of creating, with Jesus, a new society. Such was the Christmas message and gift of liberation proclaimed by Father Grande on that Advent Sunday in 1975.

Priestly Anniversary of Archbishop Chávez y González

When 13-year-old Rutilio Grande met Archbishop Luis Chávez

y González on a pastoral visit made to El Paisnal, the young Rutilio accompanied the archbishop on his trips to the outlying towns. Their early encounter set the foundation for a lifelong friendship between Grande and the archbishop. In later years, Rutilio would refer to the archbishop as his spiritual father and the one who helped him realize his priestly call. At 39, Chávez y González was the youngest archbishop to be appointed in El Salvador. In 1974, when he celebrated his golden anniversary of priesthood, Grande invited him to Aguilares for a special anniversary Mass. As pastor of the parish, Rutilio used the occasion to gather the lay ministers who had been formed in the two years since he and his Jesuit team members had assumed responsibility of Our Lord of Mercies parish. Opening his sermon, Rutilio shared his memory of that youthful encounter with Archbishop Chávez y González.

> I was only a child of thirteen years old, when Monseñor, a young archbishop of 39 years, came through here on his first pastoral visit, meeting me as I journeyed on the path of my life: It was the explicit and visible confirmation of the priestly vocation that I had been feeling in my interior for years. He called me in the name of the Lord and I followed him on the way to the Seminary...[18]

Acknowledging the presence of not only his brother priests but also the lay Delegates of the Word present at the anniversary Mass, Rutilio expressed gratitude not only for his priestly calling, but also for their role in his priestly growth.

> [They]...encourage me in my priesthood, with their fervor, their love for Christ, their courage and their desire to build new communities, according to the spirit of the Gospel. And more concretely, with their frequent and many trips from place to place, with their sleepless nights, and poor eating, because of the multiple meetings in which they engage, either in their own communities, or by coming to this parish seat. And all, because of the Gospel.[19]

As the best tribute that could be given to the archbishop celebrating his golden priestly anniversary, Grande offered the fruitfulness of the innovative pastoral endeavor in Aguilares: the establishment of 47 communities in the city and surrounding countryside, 200 marriages blessed, 1157 baptisms performed,[20] 500 first communions with the preparation given by fifty catechists. Grande emphasized, however, that numbers do not equal pastoral success. If the people in the parish are not properly evangelized, the sacraments are empty rituals that neither correspond to lived realities, nor enable men and women to change a world in rapid decomposition. Although evangelization as urged by Pope Paul VI and demanded by the Gospel is difficult, nevertheless, it is a fundamental necessity. In giving tribute to the archbishop through the anniversary Mass, Father Grande concluded by asking his beloved spiritual father and mentor to bless the ministers who give themselves to the service of the community.

Soledad (Our Lady of Solitude)

For Rutilio the liturgy provided a profound source of prayer. His few surviving reflections written on Holy Thursday or Good Friday reveal his deep devotion to the Eucharist and other liturgical celebrations. Holy Week inspired him to write letters or poetic reflections on the mysteries of that liturgical season. His files contained a Good Friday reflection addressed to Our Lady of Solitude (*Soledad*). Beautifully expressed and poetic, it is easy to imagine Father Rutilio sitting at his desk in the rectory at Aguilares after the Good Friday services, placing himself in the presence of Mary and sharing the sense of solitude that she most likely experienced on that Good Friday many centuries ago. That intuition of her solitude, of being left alone, is evoked in the opening lines:

They are gone, Mother, they have left you alone.
Alone with the child in your arms like as on that
Night in Bethlehem! They are all gone:
Soldiers and Pharisees,
Merchants and daughters of Jerusalem,
Apostles…

All the rabble
All of humanity
Gone down to Jerusalem
With them we have all gone.
For ourselves as well
Good Friday
But a moment…
Afterwards we return to the same.
Above at the top of the hill,
You are alone, Mother.
Alone with your Son in your arms
The rest of us
Have returned to town.[21]

In this meditation, as in all his various modes of communication, Grande was conscious of the social context and reality of the country and of those to whom he provided spiritual leadership. Reflecting on Good Friday, a religious celebration so deeply embedded in the spiritual and cultural ethos of the Salvadoran people, he evoked the human struggle being played out in his times.[22] Rutilio connected the scriptural figures of Pilate, Caiaphas and of the servant Malchus to the behaviors and actions of his contemporary men and women.

Like Pilate, most of us, have washed our hands
when we see the suffering of God and human beings,
and we calm our conscience
while making deals with God and the devil,
doing what God wants and what we want.
Those of us who know how to climb the ladder of success
and like to be on top at all costs,
those of us who like to separate business from life,
those who pretend to be a good Christian,
but keep asking Christ "What is the truth?"
We leave swiftly so we don't really hear an answer.
We like to be on top occupying high positions,
playing our cards with both Christ and Barabbas,
and wash our hands one more time.[23]

Concluding, Father Grande appealed to Our Lady of Solitude for her compassion and understanding.

Don't judge us too badly
for leaving you alone with the dead Christ.
You will see on the third day, when we find out He is risen,
we will again believe in Him, us, poor Christians that we are.
When things are not that hard,
you will see how we all return to you:
Peter, the daughters of Jerusalem,
and perhaps even the gatekeeper's priest
and Malchus the servant.
And you, Mother, will smile upon us again,
you will pretend that you didn't notice
that we left you all alone this very afternoon
on Good Friday.[24]

It is left to speculation, whether Father Rutilio meant this to be only a personal reflection or if he shared it with the parish community. In any event, he carefully saved it in his personal files as he had written it on that Good Friday. This evocative elegy to Soledad is a rich reflection for all those who seek truth.

Published sermons

Father Rutilio's personal spirituality and innovative ministry was deeply rooted in the popular faith of the people. In Aguilares, he insisted that the work of the pastoral team be shaped by the people's faith. Rutilio's exceptional gift in this area was evidenced in his transformation of traditional religious and cultural celebrations. His surviving sermons speak to this gift of connecting with the populace.

Feast of the Transfiguration

Rutilio Grande's earliest published homily was delivered on 6 August 1970, El Salvador's patronal feast of the Divine Savior of the World (Divino Salvador del Mundo), which is celebrated in El Salvador on the Feast of the Transfiguration. At the time, social tensions revolving around issues of agrarian land reform fueled internal tensions within the Church of El Salvador. The Second Vatican Council's strong call for renewal both within the Church and in its relationship to the modern world presented new challenges for the bishops in Latin America:

> The joys and the hopes, the griefs and the anxieties of the men [and women] of this age, especially those who are poor or in any way afflicted, these are the joys and hopes, the griefs and anxieties of the followers of Christ. (Gaudium et Spes, §1)

The 1968 Conference of Latin American Bishops in Medellín drew attention to both the stark reality of the overwhelming poverty in their countries and the urgency to develop a new course of evangelization. At a meeting in Guatemala in 1970, the Central American Bishops committed themselves to implementing the conclusions of the Second Vatican Council and of the Council of Medellín.

Despite these high aspirations, in actuality, the bishops of El Salvador were not ready for such change. During the First National Pastoral Week held in July 1970 in San Salvador to implement the directions of Medellín, the conclusions reached by the general assembly of pastoral ministers were rejected by the bishops. Consequently, the final document contained no reference to either the Vatican Council or Medellín. The bishops' revisionist stance profoundly distressed Rutilio Grande. He felt obligated to address the full assembly, asking them to support the original conclusions. His actions, however, compromised his personal good standing with the bishops.

Surprisingly, however, it was Grande whom the Salvadoran bishops shortly thereafter invited to preach in the Cathedral on the Feast of the Transfiguration, celebrating the Divine Savior of the World, El Salvador's patronal feast. Annually the patronal celebration in the capital city brought together political representatives, ecclesial hierarchy, clergy, religious, and lay men and women. To be invited to give the homily at this cultural and religious event was considered an honor.

Although those who lived with Rutilio in the parish of Our Lord of Mercies in Aguilares were aware of how much it cost him to present himself in such a broad public setting, he accepted the invitation. Afflicted by the usual distress and lack of confidence that disconcerted him in such situations, Rutilio nevertheless meticulously and conscientiously prepared the homily.

Given the controversial makeup of the congregation, he repeatedly reviewed the adequacy and appropriateness of what he had written. He began the homily with the question: "Why are we here?" offering the congregation several specious responses for that challenging question.

> Am I here because this is a Mass that I would never miss or the religious ritual of the descent of the Divine Savior, on the afternoon of the 5th of August? That and the processions of Holy Week, I never miss them. Everything else I don't care about. I show up at church every once in a while; but I do not have clear ideas of what the reality of Christianity is all about nor about the gospel of Jesus as it relates to my own life in regard to my country and the entire world. All the rest I don't worry about![25]

His question challenged the assembly to further explore what it meant to be a committed Christian in the real world and how that commitment was essential to the authentic celebration of the Eucharist. Directing his words to everyone gathered in the Cathedral, both the civic and ecclesial authorities, he pressed them to consider the heart of the question. He highlighted the three words of the Salvadoran national motto—God, Union, Liberty—asking whether these values had been actualized for the people in El Salvador.[26]

He then turned their attention to the Scriptural role of Jesus: the prophet who entered fully into the lives of men and women of His times to proclaim the good news and denounce evil, Jesus as liberator of those who suffer. In denouncing the evil of His time, Christ died: a challenge for the Church and for all the baptized. In a Catholic country such as El Salvador, where everyone considered themselves baptized, Rutilio took and expanded that cultural religious norm.

> We all confess ourselves as baptized, the sons [and daughters] of this nation. Our governors, the ministers of the state, the intellectuals and professionals, the employed, the military, tradespeople are baptized; all our campesinos are bap-

tized, and before everything else all the priests, bishops, religious men and women are baptized.[27]

He reminded the ecclesiastical and political authorities:

> The Church in its sphere, and the Government in what belongs to them, with mutual respect within their legitimate areas, must collaborate effectively, boldly, and urgently in order to promote 'just laws, that are honest and convenient,' as required by the sovereignty of the people in the first article of the Constitution.[28]

In his conclusion, he urged the Church and the government:

> [T]o transform the Salvadoran people living in the valleys, beside the beautiful lakes, along the Lempa River, at the edge of the flowering coffee plantations and channels, on the slopes of our mountains and volcanoes, in the villages and hamlets and the large growing urban concentrations and beside the large landholdings.[29]

He left them with a challenge: only by addressing the real concerns of the people of El Salvador would the patronal feast of the Divine Savior of the World become an authentic expression of faith, not an empty cultural gesture. Throughout this homily, he wove together the actual reality of the people with the timely reality of a prophetic message.

Following this sermon, Rutilio Grande received the two vastly different responses: a positive one from the President of the Republic, and a critical one from the Salvadoran bishops. While President Fidel Sánchez congratulated him with the promised gift of a copy of the *Constitution of the Republic of El Salvador*, the bishops frowned upon not only the content of the sermon but also Grande's specific references to their role and posture.[30]

Third Festival of the Corn

An annually-occurring cultural celebration was *La Fiesta del Maíz* honoring corn as a primary source of sustenance for the people of El Salvador. Understanding its importance and popular significance, Grande creatively developed the celebration to honor not only Mary, the Mother of God, but also by extension all Salvadoran women, especially the poor women of the rural communities. Praising the value of rural (peasant) women as the perfect embodiment of "*nuestro pueblo*" (our people) he called attention not only to women, but also to the sacredness of corn as the primary sustenance of the land. For the parish celebration, he invited each community to bring and share food made from corn. Each community was asked to present a creative representation of the many uses of corn; for example, a song in praise of corn or a decoration accenting its natural beauty. In addition, each community named a godmother, a woman selected for her service and efforts on behalf of the community. Rutilio put the finishing touch to the celebration by delivering a sermon that highlighted the power in Mary's Magnificat and extolled the importance of women and their communities.[31]

During his time as pastor of the parish of Our Lord of Mercies in Aguilares, Rutilio celebrated three Festivals of the Corn (1974, 1975, 1976). These celebrations of the Festival of the Corn captured the campesinos' experience of the value of community. The formation implemented by the pastoral team was aimed at developing men and women committed to gospel justice and equality for all. The insights fostered by the process of evangelization led many of the campesinos to organize themselves politically to confront the injustices that oppressed them. It is in this context of advanced pastoral formation that the celebration of the third Festival of the Corn took place on 16 August 1976.

Grande's sermon was not limited to the liturgically assigned moment following the Gospel. Instead it threaded its way throughout the entire celebration. Throughout the liturgy, he used the language, the colloquial expressions and images commonly used by the campesinos. From the beginning welcome, Father Rutilio's words illuminated each moment of the Eucharist. All those in attendance were drawn into full participation, and male and female representatives of the diverse communities were actively involved in the liturgical moments. One male campesino spoke on behalf of the communities to praise Mary and the women campesinas. Although the actual contributions of the participants are not recorded in the copy of Grande's sermon, they are included in the schema of the sermon.

A year earlier, El Salvador had hosted the Miss Universe Pageant. So for the Eucharist of the second Festival of the Corn, Grande grounded the theme in the spirit of the Magnificat. He critiqued the secular and commercial beauty pageant that exalted women for their physical looks, for the common practice of buying votes to win, and for the grand parties at the Sheraton hotel.

He contrasted those pampered women with the campesina women who had been chosen to represent their rural communities at the festival because of the many ways that they served their communities. Theirs, he contended, was the authentic beauty to which the Salvadoran women should aspire and celebrate. And above all, Mary the Mother of God was chosen by God as the truly beautiful woman, a beauty that did not require her waist to be measured, or as Rutilio popularly said: "… María is the one that has been chosen for centuries as Queen, as a beautiful woman, because she need not have a wasp-like waist measurement to meet the measure of beauty."[32] Anyone who lived in El Salvador would have recognized Rutilio's clear cultural and societal allusions.

Grande not only extolled Mary, but also pointed out that God will always have mercy on those who fear him. And how is one to identify those who do not fear the LORD? Father Grande identified those who did not fear the LORD. They were the ones who, making the sign of the cross, prayed "In the name of the coffee, in the name of coffee and in the name of coffee…!! In the name of the sugarcane, in the name of the sugarcane, and in the name of the sugarcane."[33] The campesinos at the Mass would have clearly understood Rutilio's unvarnished reference to the wealthy landowners who were their employers.

Turning his attention to the leaders in local communities, he praised their wonderful efforts in dedicating themselves to the betterment of their communities and to evangelization. Grande reminded them that faith is expressed through words and deeds. He referenced the popular refrain of a church hymn that proclaimed that prayer alone was not sufficient (*no basta rezar*). He underscored the intimate link between prayer and active engagement in the world. In addition, local efforts extended beyond the parish with a global reach. Care and dedication to all one's actions was important, nothing should be carelessly done. The formation of children, baptismal preparation, and the roles of the Delegate of the Word and Catechists, were all vital to the Christian life and baptismal commitment. He made special mention of a group of elderly men from El Paisnal dedicated to the Adoration of the Blessed Sacrament who at great sacrifice had put aside old practices and accepted a new understanding of evangelization. Rutilio emphatically reminded everyone of their personal responsibility in the selection of parish leadership.

> One cannot play with the responsibility of community elections on which depends the vitality of the Church in each village or canton. I ask you to strive for the deep study of Sacred Scripture in your global process of salvation history[34] ... These studies are linked to a deep reflection with real situations of local and national events, in the country, to act.[35]

Grande also stressed the significance of the Eucharist as central in the life of the Christian community.

> It is not the taking bread like you would take corn bread.[36] Rather, it is a dynamic that comes from life, is mediated through these external signs and goes to life ... This is as much a Eucharist, as is the Festival of Corn that we will be celebrating shortly. This is as much Eucharist as is life in the canton, as life is experienced at work in the store, as lived in the struggle for human rights, or in making one's way through the parish.[37]

As Rutilio prepared for the Offertory, he highlighted the dignity and value of campesino daily life:

> We present to you Lord, these offerings, the humble tortilla, hosts of our people; corn, the sweat of our people in their vital efforts from planting to harvesting...[38]

In essence, Grande was teaching that all of life is Eucharist. As in Aguilares, the Festival of Corn and the lives of humble campesinos[39] are linked to the celebration of Eucharist, so are evangelization and life inseparably linked.

The Apopa Sermon

As mentioned earlier, only three of Grande's sermons were published. A copy of the sermon he delivered on the occasion of the Third Festival of Corn was found in his personal files. The sermon for the Feast of the Transfiguration and the Apopa Sermon were taped and later transcribed.[40] All three sermons are important, although the Apopa Sermon is often considered the most significant and the one that incited the opposition and led to Grande's death. It was written by Father Rutilio in response to the escalating expulsions of foreign religious and priests from El Salvador.

The economic and social disintegration in the country created a dire situation of overall agitation. For the first time, El Salvador had a regional trade deficit and its general foreign trade diminished precipitously. Every day brought news of kidnappings, extortion, murders and expulsions. Discontent grew among the citizenry, but negative developments were facilely ascribed to an insidious threat of communist infiltration. Pastoral work carried out in places such as that in Aguilares were regarded with suspicion. Catechists, delegates of the Word, and active Christians became the targets of repression. At the end of January 1977, Father Mario Bernal, originally from Colombia, South America, and pastor in the town of Apopa, was kidnapped, tortured, and then expelled from El Salvador.

Father Bernal belonged to the Ecclesial Vicariate of Quezaltepeque; consequently, the Church in San Salvador took urgent action to publicly protest his mistreatment and expulsion. The clergy and lay ministers working in that vicariate designated Rutilio Grande to be the spokesperson for the "manifestation of faith," that was planned to denounce the abuse of church ministers.

Grande's homily delivered in Apopa on 13 February 1977, decried the numerous abuses that were being unleashed upon innocent people simply because they carried a Bible or spoke in the name of Jesus. Rutilio did not accept the rationale that

Father Bernal was expelled from the country because he was a "foreigner." He refuted that pretext in the Apopa homily.

> They tell me that he was a foreigner! Father Mario, a foreigner?! Certainly... and from Latin America. I wonder how in Latin America, discovered by Columbus where we are all kneaded together with coffee and milk as well as blood, we can be foreigners! Can we be foreigners anywhere?[41]

Posing the fundamental question, he asked, how does one live as a Christian in a world of such injustice? His homily courageously rebuked the few who held the economic wealth of the country in their hands.

> It is not a matter that I say, "I bought half of El Salvador with my money, therefore it is my right and there is no right to discuss!" It is a purchased right, because I have the right to buy half of El Salvador. It is a negation of God! There is no right that counts before those of the people! ...Therefore the material world is for everyone, without borders. Therefore, a communal table with long tablecloths like this Eucharist is for everybody. Each one with a seat at the table. And let there be for everybody table, tablecloths, and food.[42]

The equality of all God's children, Grande's deep held conviction, drove the Apopa sermon as it did so many of his homilies. He often referred to the communal table where everyone had a place and a right to the banquet. For those assembled at Apopa, these words were a familiar theme. Grande also underscored the importance of the Church's presence in the gathering.

> At least to give a symbolic and official demonstration of protest from the Church, from our communities, from this part of the Church Archdiocese. He [Mario Bernal] was a priest in the local Church of San Salvador and specifically here, he was the pastor of Apopa, thus having a mission on behalf of the Church in this community.[43]

Grande also made it clear that the Church was more than the

bishops, priests and religious. In the Apopa sermon, he spoke to this dimension:

> We are part of a church formed by laypeople—you are the majority of God's people. And if we have climbed here on these stands, the only purpose for our ministry is to serve you. The word 'minister' comes from 'to minister', meaning to serve God's people. From the Pope to the Bishops to the last country priest, we are servants in the community that is God's people. (Ibid.)

Father Rutilio also acknowledged that there was danger in living as a committed Christian in a country experiencing such violence and injustice. In powerful words, he tells those assembled:

> It is dangerous to be Christian in our midst! It is dangerous to be truly Catholic! It is practically illegal to be an authentic Christian here, in our country. Because out of necessity the world around us is rooted on an established disorder, in front of which the mere proclamation of the Gospel becomes subversive. (Ibid.)

No one is safe, not even Jesus:

> I fear that if Jesus tried to cross the border, there by Chalatenango, they would not let him enter! They would arrest him by Apopa...They would bring him in front of many Supreme Courts for being unconstitutional and subversive. (Ibid.)

He continued by citing the abundant signs of just how dangerous it was to be a Christian. Not only was Father Mario mistreated for proclaiming the gospel, but laity and priests had been mistreated and in some cases killed. Father Rutilio delineated a litany of such cases:

> ...Father Ivan, was brutally murdered with another North American priest and group of peasants, by a group of landowners in Olancho, Honduras...Father Hector Gallego was captured in the middle of the night in his small shack, in Santa Fé de Veraguas, Panama...a Salesian priest and a Jesuit who had defended the indigenous people

of Brazil [were killed]. In Paraguay, an irrational dictator has exiled a number of priests...A few days ago one of our brothers, Juan José Ramírez, was run over.[44]

Essentially, everyone had a right to long tablecloths and a table where all, whether poor or rich, had a seat. Grande celebrated the Eucharist in the streets of Apopa and the Mass ended in the parish church of Santa Catalina where Father Mario had been pastor until his exile. All this evoked the memory of Jesus who offered his own life for all. In conclusion, Father Rutilio invited those assembled in "manifestation of faith" to raise a cup and toast as an expression of love for Jesus, and a commitment to build the Kingdom, that is, the fraternity of a communal table, the Eucharist.

Only a month later—12 March 1977—Rutilio Grande was assassinated. In the aftermath of his murder, many speculated that the Apopa sermon contributed to the rising discontent and anger of those who felt challenged by Grande's words.

Perspective

The copies of the sermons that Grande wrote merely provide a glimpse into his thinking and his profound Christian conviction. Although it is unfortunate that only a few complete drafts exist, they offer an entry into his pastoral and theological world.

Two elements strongly influenced his ability to communicate with the people. He was born in the small town of El Paisnal among people who not only tended the fields but also were no strangers to poverty. As a child, he shared the deprivation often experienced in these rural communities. At the same time, Rutilio was immersed in the popular lived realities of the town. His was a life that followed the rhythm of campesino life—the cycle of seasons and crops—and the cultural and religious holidays and rituals that accompanied each. In El Paisnal, the young Rutilio grew up speaking the language of the people filled with images and references familiar to those raised in this rural world. Later, during his years of seminary formation and Jesuit life, Rutilio entered a much wider world opened through education and experiences in Europe and other parts of Latin America.

The advantages of these years enriched his life beyond measure, and nourished his intellectual and pastoral curiosity. Both settings shaped his ability to communicate with a broad sector of the world both at home and abroad. As a child from El Paisnal, Grande never lost the ability to speak as the common people of rural communities. At the same time, his academic preparation positioned him to be able to engage audiences that were educationally privileged.

His sermons demonstrate his ability to adapt himself to his audience. When the circumstances called for it, his words would embody the experience of peasant people. But Father Rutilio always grounded the reality of human beings in the Gospel message. He was keenly aware of the significance of history as it unfolded. Always aware of the realities of the moment, he spoke in a timely manner relevant to a specific situation so that the Gospel came alive to deliver a prophetic message.

One need only consider the context that framed the sermon protesting the eviction of the people from stalls in the Marketplace, or the Apopa sermon. Both were written and delivered as a result of a specific event. Rutilio Grande had a great sense of history and a conviction that the Gospel was intimately linked to it. Reading his sermons, one can find links to contemporary happenings, such as asking for people to "pray for the bishops that yesterday were expelled (thrown out) from Ecuador, Monseñor Proaño and bishops faithful to the Lord"[45] or his insistence that "These studies are linked to a deep reflection with real situations of local and national events, in the country, in order to act."[46] The Lord incarnated in history lived in the heart of Rutilio Grande and in his efforts to promote the Gospel.

NOTES

1. Interview with Salvador Carranza, 6 May 2014.
2. *Bendición de Un Nuevo Pabellon de la Escuela de El Paisnal* (APCSJ). Spanish citation: Vengo a bendecir una obra para bien del pueblo…Ojalá que cada día se abra una escuela en el país y se cierre una cantina; ojalá se cierre cada día un protíbulo y se abra una escuelita cada día en el más apartado rinconcito de nuestra tierra…Una escuela es una bendición para el pueblo por todo lo que ella simboliza.
3. Ibid. Spanish citation: Vuelvo a mis palabras inciales. Soy un dirigente Religioso y no pertenezco a ninguna facción política. Ruego muy de veras que ninguna facción me inscriba

en sus listas oficiales o archivos particulares, porque me debo al pueblo entero, en vocación de servicio y en función de unos valores eternos que coinciden con los valores fundamentales del hombre y que no son patrimonio de ningún grupo o facción. El Evangelio de Jesús, pregona esos valores, los defiende en la historia concreta del mundo y los inmortaliza con la trascendencia del más allá.

4. Ibid. Spanish citation: …la Iglesia y sus autoridades, bendecirán y alabarán todos los esfuerzos que se hagan para el bien común del pueblo…vengan de donde vengan esos logros o esfuerzos. Porque como he dicho y lo repito, la Iglesia es portadora de los más puros valores del Evangelio que coinciden con las más profundan aspiraciones humanas…

5. *La Bendición de Una Escuela*, no date (APCSJ). Spanish citation: La palabra bendición se deriva etimológicamente de la palabra Latina "benedicere" que significa "decir o desear el bien" sobre personas y cosas. Desear la salud, la prosperidad, la buena cosecha, el éxito en las empresas, en fin todo aquello que redunda en bien del hombre… Cada transformación de la tierra y de lo que ella contiene es una bendición amplia y generosa.

6. Ibid. Spanish citation: ...no hay un esfuerzo conjunto de los hombres, hay la ambición de algunos y el mal en muchos. La maldición suprema es el pecado que anida en el corazón del hombre y corrompe grupos y comunidades enteras ...

7. Ibid. Spanish citation: …preparando a nuevas generaciones de campesinos, conscientes de su vocación de hombres libres en medio de la comunidad nacional ... Pedimos a Dios que esta escuela brille como una luz en medio de la comunidad y que los niños que comienzan sus estudios puedan hasta que llegue a las aulas universitarias, a las que todos los salvadoreños capaces tengan acceso, incluidos los humildes hijos de nuestros campesinos

8. A draft of this sermon was found in Grande's archives identified with phrase – Domingo 29 de Octubre—No year noted (APCSJ).

9. Ibid. Spanish citation: Por lo tanto, al no encontrar ningún motivo serio y válido para tales estímulos de mercado, creemos que es injusto, que es un pecado grave y escandaloso que no podemos ocultar, callar o encubrir, porque si lo hicimos, complicaríamos ese pecado público y no podemos hacerlo en conciencia ... Denunciamos esta injusticia como algo que va en contra de los derechos humanos más elementales y, naturalmente, contra el Evangelio que nosotros como bautizados tenemos que vivir y vivir.

10. Ibid. Spanish citation: Si he hablado de este hecho es porque debo defender a todo aquel que es atropellado injustamente, quienes quien que sea, incluso aunque sea hermano protestante o sin religion."

11. *Reflexion sobre el Dios de los Militares*, no date (APCSJ). Spanish citation: Oímos una serenata esta mañana, frente al templo parroquial en honor del Señor de las Miser[icordias]… Ojalá que oigamos la serenata que el Señor de las Misericordias quiere que oigamos todos cuantos nos decimos dirigentes en este país: la serenata de su EVANGELIO, que proclama los valores de la justicia, de la fraternidad, del amor, de un orden nuevo, para forjar un mundo nuevo…y para "despertar" a un cambio urgente y necesario. Hay que despertar con esa sere[nata].

12. Ibid. This is the direct Spanish citation: Tenemos que servir al pueblo y no servirnos del pueblo. Nosotros, los sacerdotes y los soldados, no debemos dejarnos comprar por un puñado de casicones para atentar contra el pueblo.

13. In a visit with Cleveland Ursuline Sisters who worked in El Salvador during the civil war, they recounted their memories of the recruitment raids carried out by military and guerrillas in the small towns of the country. This was a method used to fill the ranks of the military and popular army. This was shared with me during a dinner gathering held on 1 July 2017 in Cleveland, Ohio. Sister Dorothy Kazel who was one of the four women killed in El Salvador was a member of this Ursuline community.

14. See: Ana María Pineda, *Romero & Grande: Companions on the Journey*, 9.

15. *Navidad Campesina*, 21 December 1975 (APCSJ). Spanish citation: Ayer como Hoy, los hombres buscan a Jesús para preguntarle. ¿Eres tú el que debe venir o debemos esperar a otro?

16. Ibid., Spanish citation: Jesús, su Evangelio, nos ha abierto los ojos. Antes estabamos ciegos,

Rutilio Grande

ahora vemos nuestra realidad de injusticia y opresión. Antes estabamos sordos, ahora oímos la palabra de Dios. Antes estabamos mudos, ahora hablamos, nos defendemos, cuestionamos, no nos quedamos callados ante la injusticia. Estas son las senales que encontramos en nuestras comunidades. Deseamos y buscamos quitar la opresión, la injusticia en nosotros y en nuestras comunidades, en nuestra sociedad. Estas son las señales de que Jesús nace en nosotros.

17. Ibid. Spanish citation: Somos nosotros campesinos, sin esperanza, sin dignidad, sin posibilidades de ninguna clase dentro de esta sociedad.
18. *Homenaje al Señor Arzobispo Monseñor Luis Chávez y González, En Sus 50 Años de Sacerdocio*, Aguilares, 29 de Diciembre, 1974 (APCSJ). Spanish citation: Siendo yo todavía un niño de 13 años, Monseñor, joven Arzobispo de 39 años, pasó por aquí cerca en su primera visita pastoral, junto al camino de mi vida: Fué la confirmación de mi vocación sacerdotal que venía sintiendo en mi interior desde hacía años. El me llamó en nombre del Señor y lo seguí camino del Seminario…
19. Ibid. Spanish citation: … aquí presentes, que me estimulan en mi sacerdocio, con su fervor, con su amor por Cristo, con su valentía y con su anhelo de construir unas comunidades nuevas, según el espiritu del Evangelio. Y más concretamente, con sus frecuentes y grandes caminatas, con sus noches de desvelo, con su mal dormir y peor comer, por sus múltiples reuniones, bien sea en sus propias comunidades, bien sea encaminandose hasta esta sede parroquial. Y todo, por el Evangelio.
20. In the sermon, Grande noted that prior to their arrival in the parish, 4,042 baptisms had occurred. There had been a declined in baptisms since the Jesuits took the parish as noted in the 1,157 noted in the sermon. However, the decline is due to the fact that they were adhering to the guidelines given by the archbishop which were more pastorally appropriate but also required more preparation.
21. Rutilio Grande, in his own handwriting; Good Friday, no date (APCSJ). See complete transcription in Spanish with English translation: Ana María Pineda, *Romero & Grande: Companions on the Journey*, Lectio, 2016, 155-64.
22. To my knowledge this was a personal reflection written by Grande not meant for public sharing. However, it is imbued with his theological thinking and approach.
23. See *Romero & Grande*, 161 for English translation. Spanish citation: Los que sabemos subir, conservar un puesto a costa de todo…Los que decimos que el negocio es el negocio y la vida es la vida…Los que pretendiendo ser buenos cristianos, preguntamos un día a Cristo ¿Qué es la verdad? Pero luego nos escurrimos rápidamente para no oír la respuesta. Los que con tal de estar arriba, en el alto balcón, jugamos lo mismo las cartas de Cristo y Barrabás…y siempre nos queda en ultimo término, la salida de la jarra y de la palangana en los brazos.
24. Ibid. 163-64. Spanish citation: Y no nos juzgues demasiado mal por haberte dejado sola con tu Cristo muerto. Ya veras al tercer día, cuando nos enteremos de que ha resucitado, volveremos a creer en El los pobrecitos Cristianos de siempre. Cuando la cosa esté menos fea, ya verás cómo vamos volviendo todos: Pedro, las hijas de Jerusalén…y quien sabe si hasta la portera del pontífice y el siervo de Malco. Y tú Madre, nos volverás a sonreír a todos, y harás como si no te hubieras dado cuenta de que te hemos dejado sola esta tarde de Viernes Santo.
25. See Ana María Pineda, *Romero & Grande*, 98.
26. Ibid.
27. Ibid., 99
28. Ibid.
29. Ibid.
30. This portion which addresses Grande's sermon delivered on the Feast of the Transfiguration is taken from my book: *Romero & Grande: Companions on the Journey*, 96-99.
31. See: Ana María Pineda, *Romero & Grande*, 77.
32. *Misa Solemne Popular: Tercer Festival de Maíz*. August 15 (APCSJ). Spanish citation: … que ha sido elegida por los siglos como reina, como la Mujer bella y tipa, porque no le irán a tomar medidas de cintura de avispa.

Chapter 1

33. See: Rutilio Grande, "Homilia en el tercer festival del maíz," in XXV Aniversario, 63. Spanish citation: ...en el nombre del café, en el nombre del café y en el nombre del café. En el nombre de la caña, en el nombre de la caña y en nombre de la caña.
34. *Misa Solemne Popular: Tercer Festival de Maiz* (APCSJ) Spanish citation: no pueden jugar con cargos de elección comunitaria en los que depende la vitalidad de la Iglesia en cada pueblo o cantón. Yo les pido que se esfuercen por el estudio profundo de la Sagrada Escritura en su proceso global de historia de la Salvación .
35. Ibid. Spanish citation: Estos estudios van unidos a una reflexión profunda con situaciones reales del acontecer local y nacional, en el país, para poder actuar.
36. The word *marquesote* is used in the original. It is particular to El Salvador, and might be similar to what is known as corn bread with cheese ingredient.
37. *Misa Solemne Popular: Tercer Festival de Maíz* (APCSJ) Spanish citation: No es un tomar un pan como se toma un marquesote. Es un proceso que viene de la vida, atraviesa por estos signos exteriores y va a la vida-...Tan eucaristia es esto, como lo es tambien el festival del Maiz, que vamos a tener. Tan eucaristia es esto, como la vida en el canton, como la vida en el trabajo en la tienda, como la lucha por los derechos humanos, alli en el caminar por la parroquia. Tan eucaristia es esto, como la organización bien llevada.
38. Ibid. Spanish citation: Al presentarte, Señor estas ofrendas, la humilde tortilla, hostias de nuestro pueblo; el maíz, sudor de nuestra gente en su proceso vital desde la siembra hasta la cosecha..."
39. It is important to note that a generous portion of this section is taken from my book: Romero & Grande: Companions on the Journey, pp. 100-101. Some additional material from the original sermon of the Third Festival of Corn has been included.
40. Interview with Salvador Carranza, 6 May 2014.
41. See "Homilía de Apopa," in *XXV Aniversario de Rutilio Grande. Sus homilias*, 79. Spanish citation: Me dicen que era un extranjero! ¡¿Qué el padre Mario era extranjero?! Ciertamente, y de América Latina, descubierta por Colón, y en la que estamos todos amasados de café con leche y sangre de la misma forma, somos extranjeros! ¿Es que somos extranjeros en alguna parte?
42. Ibid. 76. Spanish citation: ¡No es cuestión que diga yo!: "Yo compré la mitad de El Salvador con mi dinero, luego tengo derecho y no hay derecho para discutir¡". Es un derecho comprado, porque tengo derecho a comprar la mitad de El Salvador. ¡No hay ningún derecho que valga ante las mayorías! Luego el mundo material es para todos, sin fronteras. Luego una mesa común con manteles largos para todos, como esta Eucaristía. Cada uno con su taburete, y que para todos llegue la mesa, el mantel y el "conqué.
43. It is important to note that a generous portion of this section is taken from my book: *Romero & Grande: Companions on the Journey*, pp. 124-27. Additional references and inclusion of the Apopa Sermon enrich this section.
44. Ibid. 84. Spanish citation: El año pasado un joven sacerdote, colombiano como tú, el padre Ivan, murió brutalmente asesinado con otro padre norteamericano y un grupo de campesinos por un grupo de terratenientes en Olancho, Honduras...el Padre Héctor Gallego fue capturado en la noche en su chocita, allá en Santa Fe de Veraguas, Panamá...a un padre salesiano y a un jesuita por defender a los indios. Y, en Paraguay, han sido desterrados por un dictador irracional varios sacerdotes...Hace unos días, Juan José Ramírez...un hermano nuestro, acaba de ser atropellado.
45. *Misa Solemne Popular: Tercer Festival de Maíz* (APCSJ). Spanish citation: Oramos con los obispos que ayer fueron expulsados del Ecuador, Monseñor Proaño y los obispos fieles al Señor.
46. Ibid. Spanish citation: Esos estudios van unidos a una reflexión profunda con situaciones reales del acontecer local y nacional, en el país, para poder actuar.

CHAPTER 2

THE PRESS

During his seminary years, the young Rutilio (pictured here as a first-year seminarian) received an education that he would not have had if he had remained in El Paisnal. In 1963-64 he studied in Belgium at Lumen Vitae. The experience not only exposed him to the latest catechetical methods of the time, such as the See-Judge-Act method, but also acquainted him with the leading experts in the field. Then in 1972, Grande was sent to the Latin American Pastoral Institute (IPLA) in Quito, Ecuador. These educational opportunities in Belgium and Quito placed him at the center of innovative pastoral and theological approaches which had been inspired by the Second Vatican Council and Medellín. Both study experiences provided rich exchanges with internationally known theologians and pastoralists.

As a result, Rutilio's use of the See-Judge-Act method took on a real vitality. He understood the urgent need to address the interconnection between Church and society. Coupled with his ability to communicate the Gospel in the context of the real human experiences, Father Rutilio frequently contributed to the local newspapers, *Prensa Gráfica* and *El Mundo*. A letter written to Rosalio Hernández, the editor of *Prensa Gráfica*, reveals that

Rutilio wrote several articles for that local newspaper: "Lexicología y Cristianismo de Todos Los Tiempos" (Lexicology and Christianity of All Time), 27 July 1970; "A Propósito de Una Bendición" (For the Purpose of a Blessing), 31 July 1970; "La verdad os hará libres" (The Truth will set you free) no date; "Religion, Opio del pueblo?" (Religion, Opium of the People?) 21 August 1970.

Grande also authored several articles for another local newspaper, *El Mundo*. In May of 1970 his series of four articles focused on the social realities of El Salvador: "Lo Social también es de Compentencia de la Iglesia" (The Social is also of the Competence of the Church); "Realidades y Justicia" (Realities and Justice); "Realidad social Salvadoreña" (Salvadoran Social Reality); "Violencia sangrienta y Violencia Institucionalizada" (Bloody Violence and Institutionalized Violence). Copies of these articles were kept in his personal files.

Provocatively, Grande opens the series with the article "Lo Social también es de Competencia de la Iglesia" acknowledging that the title would cause some consternation. He writes that there are those who believe

> that the priest must remain in the sacristy, talk of love and charity, teach the children doctrine, give them vouchers for the parochial cinema and distribute among the needy the alms that the faithful give him. They think that the priest must be a good man who does not go where he is not called.[1]

Rutilio conceded that although there are those who ascribe to this belief, it is not correct. He explains that the role of the priest is to engage in the dynamic in which people live day-to-day. He references the social teachings of the Church to substantiate his perspective. "From the time of Leo XIII," he wrote, "we have seen a remarkable insistence on the fact that economic questions cannot be dissociated from morality." He cited the teachings of Pope Pius X: "The social question and the controversies of it, based on the nature and duration of work, on the amount of wages, on the voluntary strike of the workers, are not exclusively moral and religious in nature." Furthermore, Pope Pius

XI insisted that the object of morality [nevertheless] included the object of the economy, and that it was erroneous to believe that they were not linked. Ultimately, Father Rutilio affirmed that the Church cannot separate the economy from what affects humankind who are, above all, the concern of the Church. In the words of Pope Paul VI: "Economics and technology have no meaning if it is not for the man they should serve."

The following week, Grande wrote "Realidades y Justicia," the second article in the *El Mundo* series. In his opening, he states the purpose of the article:

> The social realities of Latin America lend themselves to multiple reflections, attitudes and reactions. We want to reflect objectively, take rational attitudes and react not in favor of changes in structure, but rather in the conversion of people whose demands can bring about change with the assistance of technical skills.[2]

> What is needed are people who understand the necessity for change while combating its greatest enemy—human egoism. Consequently, the important task is the preparation and formation of those who, without personal interests, will fight for justice and human development.

In order to shed light on the need for societal changes in Latin America, Rutilio highlighted significant statistics to make his point. The population alone was projected to triple from 200 million in 1960 to 690 million in 2000. The population explosion contributed to a growing number of challenges facing the country: 1) 40% of the population were under fifteen years of age and not significantly able to contribute to the development of society; 2) 53.4% represented the rural sector whose low wages made minimal monetary contribution to the country; 3) less than 10% of the population enjoyed more than 60% of the national product; 4) the unequal distribution of land, with the bulk in the hands of the wealthy, created unequal access for the majority of the poor; and finally 5) the alarming deficit of housing could not meet the needs of the rapidly growing population.[3] Having highlighted Latin America's pertinent statistics, Grande concluded with a challenge to his readership:

> These are some facts, not all. But they speak of great needs, of marked inequalities within and outside Latin America, of complicated national and international problems ... We do not ignore the complexity of the solutions, especially in the area of international trade and finance, but neither do we ignore that it is a great crime against man and mankind to remain with our arms crossed because problems are complicated.[4]

In order to make justice a reality, Father Rutilio considered it a duty to try to raise consciousness among persons of goodwill who had the skills to look for solutions.

Realidad social Salvadoreña

On Thursday, 14 May 1970, the third article of the *El Mundo* series was published: "Realidad social salvadoreña." Grande quoted the Second Vatican Council:

> God has designed the earth and everything it contains for the use of the whole human race. Consequently, the goods created must reach all in a just way, under the aegis of justice and with the company of charity. Therefore, in using (goods), man should not have the external things that he legitimately possesses as exclusively his own, but also held in common, in the sense that they do not benefit him alone, but also others.[5]

In an earlier article, Rutilio had provided information on the realities of Latin America. He then examined some of the social aspects related specifically to El Salvador beginning with the density of a population living in such a small territory. The median age was sixteen. The youthfulness of the population brought with it corresponding problems to provide food, housing, health and education for them. In the area of education alone, half of the population was illiterate. Illiteracy was an enormous challenge not only for the current population but for the growing future population. Over 1,377,000 persons were without decent housing. The per capita income was minuscule as Salvadorans earned a meager $153 USD per year. According to the data of the second agricultural census of 1961, the distribution of land required serious attention as the number of large estates overwhelmed the number of small holdings, thereby increasing homelessness especially for those living in rural areas.[6]

In light of all these social factors, Grande presented a lengthy list of steps which would be required to respond to the country's dire social needs.

> Comprehensive agrarian reform, including the exploitation of uncultivated land, sanitation and exploitation of existing ones, is urgently needed, crop selection, overcoming monoculture, industrialization of agricultural products, increasing domestic and international markets, credit assistance at low interest to the farmer and fiscal aid, roads of communication, tax and credit assistance to the agricultural industry, international credit, agricultural cooperatives and above all, education and vocational training for the *campesino*.[7]

Rutilio concluded the article with a litany of the economic and social factors plaguing the country. While he does not return to the opening quote from the Second Vatican Council, he leaves it to the reader to draw their own conclusion.

Violencia sangrienta y Violencia Institucionalizada

The final article of Grande's series was published on 19 May 1970. In it, Grande acknowledged the tragedy of the cycle of bloody violence that Latin America was suffering, a violence which Pope St. Paul VI condemned as neither Christian nor evangelical. It became increasingly clear that armed violence had to be examined in the light of social injustice. Accordingly, Rutilio sees the

> ... situation of injustice that can be called institutionalized violence when, due to the structures of industrial and agricultural enterprise, national and international economy, cultural and political life, entire populations lack the necessities of life, live in such a dependency that prevents any initiative and responsibility, as well as any possibility of cultural promotion and participation

in social and political life, thus violating fundamental rights. Such a situation demands global transformations, that is bold, urgent and deeply renovating.[8]

No forms of violence, neither institutional nor armed, can support a peace that is born of justice as envisioned by the Second Vatican Council. Violence is a complex situation. It can be interpreted in multiple ways. In order to provide a solid framework for the reader, Grande used statistical data to demonstrate the serious gap of earned income between the struggling masses (60%—130 colones per month equivalent to $14.00 USD) and the wealthier families (8%—400 colones per month equivalent to $45.71 USD). The majority of the population spend approximately 12 colones (equivalent to $1.37 USD) per month as opposed to 58% spending 24 colones ($2.74 USD) per month.[9] The message was clear. There can be no peace unless there is a just distribution of goods. Although the problem is complex, it is the responsibility of those who have the power to use their influence to bring about changes in the economy and the politics of the country.

Perspective

Grande's articles written for the local press underline his active engagement in civic matters and his belief that the daily concerns and realities of people were intimately linked to the Gospel. He indicated in an earlier article that Leo XIII had "seen a remarkable insistence on the fact that economic questions cannot be dissociated from morality."[10] Consequently, the role of the priest was not limited to the sacristy or to the mere formulaic dispensation of sacraments that were empty of meaning. Grande's use of statistical information to illuminate the existing situation of injustices was rooted in the See-Judge-Act method that was taking hold in Latin America. Accordingly, it was first necessary to have a clear, informed grasp of facts (See); secondly, the reality had to be viewed though through the lens of the gospel (Judge); and lastly, active engagement would guide believers toward the transformation of the world (Act).

In his newspaper articles, Rutilio addressed the concrete social situations of the times and felt the Christian responsibility to foster a deeper understanding of what it meant to be a committed Christian. He availed himself of many forms of communication, not limiting himself to the parish setting. He was a gifted communicator in many forums who used his skills readily, incisively, and generously.

NOTES

1. *El Mundo*, "Lo Social también es de Competencia de la Iglesia," 8 May 1970. In this and the following paragraph, the quotations from all four popes are taken from this article.
2. *El Mundo*, "Realidades y Justicia," 13 May 1970.
3. Ibid. Statistics provided in newspaper article.
4. Ibid.
5. *El Mundo*, "Realidad social Salvadoreña," 14 May 1970. See *Gaudium et Spes* §69.
6. *El Mundo*, "Realidades y Justicia," 13 May 1970.
7. *El Mundo*, "Realidad social Salvadoreña," 14 May 1970.
8. *El Mundo*, "Violencia sangriente y Violencia Institucionalizada," 19 May 1970.
9. Ibid.
10. *El Mundo*, "Lo Social también es de Competencia de la Iglesia," 8 May 1970.

CHAPTER 3

RUTILIO'S CORRESPONDENCE

The sermons, published newspaper articles, and drafts of Rutilio Grande's written remarks serve as portals into the thinking process of this native son of El Salvador, who was born into poverty and died in defense of the poor. Although his published work is limited to a few sermons, newspaper columns and some pastoral articles, his correspondence deepens our insight. Grande's correspondence falls roughly into several groupings:

1) Letters from Archbishop Chávez y González and from Rutilio Grande to Chávez;
2) Letters in which Rutilio refers to his health;
3) Letters that respond to situations in his ministry;
4) Letters in which he makes specific reference to the political realities in El Salvador;
5) Letters to Rutilio Grande from Romero and notes from Alfonso López Trujillo;
6) Letters from others regarding Rutilio and/or in reference to experiences with him;
7) Letters Rutilio exchanged with his older brother, Flavio Grande.

Archbishop Chávez y González

Thirteen-year-old Grande had met Archbishop Chávez y González, the youngest named Archbishop in the history of the church of El Salvador, during the prelate's first pastoral visit to the small hamlet of El Paisnal. The boy already was rooted in the religious life of the town through his grandmother Francisca whom he often accompanied in her care of the local church. Perhaps it was this familiarity with all that pertained to the church that made the boy a likely companion to the archbishop on that pastoral visit. Shortly afterwards, Rutilio began to correspond with the prelate, expressing a desire to become a priest. That first letter was the beginning of a life-long correspondence.

Over the years, as Rutilio remarked in a letter of 11 January 1976, he had dutifully saved all the letters, postcards, and Christmas greetings received from the archbishop.

> You know well the profound affection that I have always had for you since my childhood. Since then I have kept your many letters on file, as a testimony that proves what I say, because I have always communicated with you throughout the various stages of my life: as a child from my town, as a result of your first Pastoral Visit, as a seminarian through my five years of Seminary, and in the various periods of my formation in the Company of Jesus, to which I enter with your benevolent acquiescence.[1]

After Grande's death a carefully organized collection of the archbishop's correspondence was found in Rutilio's personal belongings. The file folder bearing the episcopal photo of the youthful archbishop contained thirty-six years of personal communication.

One of the first exchanges between the two concerned Rutilio's desire to enter the seminary and the response from the archbishop in which he counseled the young man:

> I write to you on this day when we celebrate the Day in Favor of Seminary, it is a great day since it is the feast of PENTECOST, on the day in which the Church commemorates the COMING OF THE HOLY SPIRIT, for which I beg you earnestly to ask the Holy Spirit, who is God as the Father and the Son, that if it is God's pleasure, for you to realize your holy desires to be a PRIEST.[2]

In addition, Chávez y González advised Rutilio to be sure to prepare himself by dedicating himself to his studies and to ask for additional tutoring.

Rutilio's Correspondence

The archbishop's hope to see Rutilio as a future priest for the Diocese of San Salvador did not materialize. After a few years in San José de la Montaña seminary in San Salvador, Rutilio felt called to continue his preparation for priesthood within the Society of Jesus. Chávez y González, however gave his blessing and supported Rutilio's decision (11 January 1976).

Their mutual affection and respect manifested itself throughout the years. While the archbishop maintained active correspondence with Rutilio through occasional letters, postcards and annual Christmas greetings, Rutilio never missed an occasion to remember his mentor and friend on special days marking the archbishop's patronal feast day or anniversaries of his priestly commitment or episcopal ordination as noted in this exchange:

> Upon my return from the Eternal City, Rome, I found your attentive letter, in which you congratulate me on the occasion of the day of my Patron Saint, St. Louis. God Our Lord will pay you for your kind remembrance and especially the spiritual bouquet offered in my name.[3]

The archbishop reciprocated his protege's attention by honoring Grande's milestones. On the eve of Rutilio's ordination, the archbishop sent a letter to Oña, Spain:

> With an affectionate and loving greeting I send you this letter on the eve of your ordination to the priesthood; with it goes my personal prayers so that God Our Lord and the Blessed Virgin Mary, save and protect you in your priesthood, for without the grace of God and the assistance of the Blessed Virgin Mary, Mother, we can do little in this sublime and incomparable state, the PRIESTHOOD.[4]

In his customary fatherly manner, the archbishop encouraged Rutilio to give himself completely over to God.

To a great extent, these letters written by Chávez y González, serve as a mirror reflecting back the interests and concerns that the two men shared and pondered. Among these topics was the question of how priestly ministry should be lived out. In the years in which Grande was in Córdoba, Spain, the archbishop shared with him the outcomes of the meetings he attended in San Salvador with particular focus on the pastoral issue of establishing and animating the Christian commitment of apostolic lay groups. They also shared their convictions regarding the continuing formation and fortification of priests. As Chávez y González expressed it: "In your prayers I beg you to pray for the priests so that they may live in the grace of God and thus be animated by the 'spirit of a true apostolate.'"[5]

For Rutilio, the mark of an authentic apostolate was the pastoral care given to those placed in the care of priests. In particular, he was most attentive to those who might be overlooked because of their marginalized place in society. One of those groups was the people in his native town of El Paisnal who were sometimes at the short end of receiving the church's pastoral attention. Grande often found himself advocating on their behalf, pleading with those in the church that they might receive more comprehensive pastoral attention. His worry is reflected in a letter in which the archbishop responded to Rutilio's concern that El Paisnal not be left without a priest: "... you must be completely tranquil, as Father José C. Pineda is currently in charge of the parish and he has special instructions to attend El Paisnal, and the seminarians continue to give the catechism."[6] As he had done so many years ago when Grande was a child,[7] Archbishop Chávez y González continued to make pastoral visits to Rutilio's home village.

Faithfully Grande kept the older man informed on his ministerial activities and projects. For some time, Rutilio had been reflecting on how to develop a ministry that could respond to the reality experienced by rural communities. He had discussed this with the Jesuit Provincial, and of course, with his spiritual father. Chávez y González's response came from Ecuador where he was attending a pastoral conference on precisely the necessity for a rural ministry.

In addition, the archbishop noted two projects being explored in El Salvador. One was the creation of a mechanism to finance the efforts carried out by religious women in parishes lacking a permanent priestly presence. The other project was the establishment of a center for formation. Both of these initiatives would have been of great interest to Grande, and the archbishop knew what to share with him.[8]

Later in 1972, the Archbishop assigned Rutilio Grande and a team of Jesuits to the pastoral responsibility of the parish of Our Lord of Mercies in the small rural town of Aguilares, which is situated in the center of El Salvador, due north of the capital city of San Salvador. While the assignment fulfilled Rutilio's longing to engage in an innovative rural pastoral plan, it also put him in charge of the mission parish of El Paisnal. As much as Grande loved his hometown, he would have preferred to be assigned to another area, but because the archbishop asked him,[9] Rutilio accepted.

The profound friendship between the two men is poignant. For almost forty years they exchanged mutually affectionate and appreciative letters. Grande considered Chávez y González key in his calling to the priesthood, as he noted in a letter that he wrote to the archbishop on 17 December 1974: "After God, I owe you my vocation as a visible instrument of the Lord's grace: Through you, He wanted to explicitly call me, the One who had chosen me for this vocation of service in His Church."[10] Freely Rutilio shared his ministerial and spiritual journey with his beloved mentor. Nevertheless, in spite of his affection and respect for the archbishop, Rutilio did not hesitate to express his opinion, as when in early 1976 he felt the need to resign as pastor from the parish in Aguilares.

As was his practice, Grande pondered the situation for some time before writing to Chávez y González: "What I am going to manifest is not the result of a flippant or immature decision, but the fruit of a long reflection, deepened first in my eight days of Spiritual Exercises made in solitude… and then continued in the course of these last months."[11]

The letter itself is a detailed explanation of the reasons why Grande felt he could no longer lead the pastoral efforts in Aguilares. He cited the growing tensions over the involvement of a group of young Jesuits in the parish who wanted to move too rapidly in the pastoral work already established by the Jesuit team. Nevertheless, as an indication of Grande's understanding of human nature, he suggested that the matter could be resolved with patience and dialogue:

> It must be taken into account that because they are young, some of them behave in their actions within the evolutionary framework proper to their age. It is possible for us adults to sin by other extremes. The truth is that I personally have been helped in a process of awareness and conversion, without this meaning that I accept all the positions of some of them without due reservation.[12]

There were a number of other reasons why Rutilio wanted to resign as pastor, which he explained in great detail to the archbishop. But true to his habitual practice, he put the final decision in the hands of his superiors. In the end, he did not resign from the parish,[13] but remained the pastor of Our Lord of Mercies until his death on 12 March 1977.

Rutilio Grande and his Health

From childhood, Grande suffered with fragile health. As a young adult, he suffered a catatonic episode (1950), which left him with chronic bouts of depression and a compromised nervous system. While this was a continual personal factor for Rutilio, he seldom talked about it. He quietly learned how to manage his tenuous health by exercising, eating well, resting, and avoiding isolation. He referenced his health condition both in his spiritual notebook and in a few letters written to Jesuit superiors.

A year after his original medical crisis, on 8 July 1951, Rutilio wrote to the Jesuit Vice-Provincial conveying improvement in his health:

> Thank God, every day I am better and better. The weight that I have gained since [the medical crisis of] Panama, helps me, as I go, for everything. I hope I will be able to maintain this weight gain at a reasonable limit. As I recall, I told V.P. that all these inspections, [teaching] classes, interactions with the seminarians, since leaving Santa Tecla and coming to the Seminary help me a lot, even regards my health.[14]

Rutilio's Correspondence

Five years after the crisis, Rutilio wrote from Oña, Spain to Agustín Bariáin, Jesuit Vice-Provincial updating his health condition:

> I went to consult with a good Psychiatrist who, after examining me for an hour and a quarter, told me that I could be completely calm. That's what I have been internally telling myself for some time now ... Physically, thank God, I'm very healthy and strong. I do not miss a field trip or a morning outing, since these walks in the mountains rest me enormously and leave me as good as new to face the following week. I methodically do gymnastics every day for a quarter of an hour when I wake up and I do very well. I sleep now for only what the community allows and with good results. I have come to consider cold weather like a benefactor: it has strengthened me; it is a wonderful stimulant of the appetite, etc. So in all this, well, as you can see. With special fervor every day I ask the Lord for the gift of good health and I believe that I am also supplying the means.[15]

The following year, 1956, he wrote to Miguel Elizondo, Jesuit Vice-Provincial:

> Apparently I am in very good health and physically robust. However, my nervous system is always weak. It is my cross. I take this into account, but I have complete confidence that I will overcome all difficulties with the help of God. The optimism that God gives me is admirable. Many times in the Novitiate I asked for a strong and heavy cross, and I never imagined that this would be my cross. I have embraced it for a long time with all its consequences ...[16]

Grande did not share the issue of his delicate health with others, not even his family; so outwardly his condition was often not apparent. "In addition everyone believes that I am already perfectly well, they see me robust and externally in good physical health and I take care not to complain or to vent, and when I do so only with those who direct me."[17]

Letters on Ministry

For Rutilio Grande, ministry was a life-long passion. Even as a child, he delighted in playing "priest" and celebrating his notion of a daily mass with the assistance of his cousins and friends. The entire town of El Paisnal was aware of "Rutilio's mass" when they heard the sounds of the bells ringing that marked the moment of "consecration." Orphaned at an early age, he was raised by his paternal grandmother and later by his older brother's wife, Lolita Grande Pineda. With his grandmother, Francisca Garcia, the young boy would go to the parish church as she took care of linens and prepared for the various ceremonies. Consequently, early on he was immersed in the life of the church and learned how to engage in pastoral service. Later in life, Grande poured his energies and talents not only into the practice of ministry, but also in creating models to serve diverse populations. He loved the church, the Society of Jesus, his family and the poor, who held a special place in his heart.

As a member of the Society of Jesus, Father Grande engaged fully in all the community endeavors, concerns and aspirations. A letter written on 14 July 1968 to Provincial Segundo Azcue exhibits Rutilio's conviction that engagement in the apostolic life nourishes the life of prayer within the community. He observed that the contemporary apostolic works of Jesuits had distanced themselves from the existing social, moral, and religious realities. He noted that the Jesuits, contrary to the genuine spirit of their Constitutions which was charac-

terized by a willingness to accept risk and to seek new perspectives,[18] were not projecting attention toward the world. In this letter to Father Azcue he contends...

> that we lack the 'apostolic-pastoral drive' in our works, a drive that is born of a pastoral vision and a congruency of action according to this vision. It was in that context that... the group of Saint Ignatius and his companions proceeded. It was what they talked about, it was their life ... It seems like that should always be the spirit which should exist in our communities.[19]

Furthermore, Grande saw his Jesuit colleagues enclosing themselves in their ministries "with little projection into the world that surrounds them, they remain isolated from the tremendous social, moral, and religious realities."[20] Reacting against what he saw as a spirit of individualism, Rutilio recommended the use of the See-Judge-Act method as a way of re-orienting Jesuit community life, spirituality, and ministry.

In fact, he was recommending for his own Jesuit brothers the approach that he had implemented in the formation of the seminarians under his charge at San José de la Montaña. As Prefect of Discipline, Father Grande was responsible for many aspects of seminary life including the appointments of those who would mentor the young seminarians in developing their spiritual life. His approach to priestly formation had been greatly influenced by his time of study at Lumen Vitae in Brussels.

As he referenced in his letter of 30 November 1969,[21] as part of the seminarians' vacation experiences, he had instituted the "Campos-Misión" models of engagement with outlying communities. Using this model, the young men spent time in the surrounding towns listening to the needs and realities of the people. Then, collating this information, they established a basis for further reflection and implementation. Based on this input and following the See-Judge-Act method, they were able to develop a process of evangelization specific to the particular communities that they visited. This innovative approach linking ministry with the people's realities in a context of faith, was accepted by some church workers yet rejected by others. The spirit of the Second Vatican Council and Medellín, which he encountered during his time at Lumen Vitae and later at IPLA, clearly both inspired and guided Grande.

Rutilio's interest embraced a variety of ministry situations. In a letter to his older brother Flavio, 19 February 1972, Rutilio shared about his time in Panama, how he was working alongside other priests who served in the area. He specifically mentioned the presence of a tribe of Guarani Indians who lived in Hato Pilón, in the high mountains of the country. Although he had already accompanied others in their ministry there, he had decided to visit this particular group on his own and to spend three days with them. He wrote:

> They are people abandoned by all: by the Church and by the government. No one goes up there, not even a priest. And the people are not baptized, and some already quite elderly! ... 15 years ago a Bishop had gone and since then a priest had not come ...[22]

To Flavio he recounted that his time there was difficult. With high altitude, it was very cold and the wind penetrated the poorly constructed huts. The food was limited and unfamiliar, but nevertheless, he accepted the challenging conditions because it was important to be present to the people. He commented to Flavio: "I would be delighted to stay here and work among those poor Indians, all my life, in order to work toward their improvement in every way."[23]

In an earlier correspondence, Grande had asked Jesuit Provincial Francisco Estrada permission to extend his visit and his experiences.

> If you have no difficulty, I would be interested in staying after the IPLA, about fifteen days in Riobamba to delve deeper into a matter of utmost importance, as this represents ... [also] I would like to spend some time again in Panama to see in detail some experiences in the light of the IPLA course.[24]

A short time afterwards, Grande wrote to Estrada, 26 February 1972, recounting ministerial experiences that he had encountered over his two months stay in South America. He had used the time to become acquainted with the apostolic activities of those living in the region. He told Estrada about his visit with the Quarani Indians, noting that they had not been attended to at all. Even work carried out in other more accessible hamlets had not engendered much response or growth, an observation that he had also communicated to Father Sosa, a Jesuit confrere who ministered there. Rutilio frankly explained to the provincial what he had proposed to Sosa.

> I told Sosa sincerely that he has to totally change method, that is, the little mass, the baptisms, and to move on in dividing the population by zones in order to form family units, holding daily meetings at night in private houses, identifying secular leaders, in a plan of carrying out a progressive evangelization that draws near to the people. Otherwise it's not worth it to be there ...[25]

On a frequent basis, Grande communicated what he was learning from his visits to other ministry sites with Estrada. He also shared his insights with others, as he had done with his Jesuit team members and the people of Aguilares when he attended a meeting of CELAM (*Conferencia Episcopal Latinoamericana*) on 24 September 1975:

> It is beautiful to note how in all our five nations of C.A. and Panama laudable efforts are being made in our Church to faithfully announce the Gospel to the different human groups of our Republics. It is the Gospel of Jesus and his energizing force (transforming) that is changing the face of our Church. I encourage you with all my personal conviction, to continue working in all our communities to understand and try to live the Gospel for the good of our peoples.[26]

His concern embraced not only the more significant movements in the Church, but also the ordinary needs of the communities such as age-appropriate bibles for children. "We are also interested in the Bible with illustrations for both children from the countryside and the city because we hold catechisms sessions throughout the year and we follow the same methodology in treating the bible."²⁷ On another occasion, he wrote to Julio López de la Puente, S.J. in Belgium requesting the purchase of breviaries for five seminarians in San Salvador who could not afford to buy them. Grande indicated that he would cover the expense.²⁸

Ministry is a recurring topic in his correspondence. On Holy Thursday, April 9, 1974 he wrote one of his most revealing letters to his Jesuit team members in Aguilares. Grande had been in route to a rural outpost for the celebration of Holy Week with the 11,000 people who lived in the surrounding hamlets when his car broke down. Forced to wait for help to arrive to repair his car, Rutilio used the time to write.

> I am writing this letter seated beneath a beautiful *amate* tree, while pigs wander around, while the roosters sing, and while I see the pale faces of children with their extended stomachs. It is 4:30 in the afternoon and shortly the people will be arriving in procession from the diverse farmhouses for the celebration of the Word of God with these humble people who are also children of God and our brothers [sisters] like the ones in Aguilares and like men [and women] from anywhere in the world.²⁹

He described the lives of the rural people—their poverty and their miserable working conditions:

> All this humble people are those taxed from Aguilares and El Paisnal, in trade and in politics. From there they go out in caravan…to work in the rich fields of sugarcane, where they leave the sweat of their work, their life and health, to earn a few miserable cents, while the owners of such immense properties place great amounts of money in banks inside and outside of the country.³⁰

> The people have no electricity and they are left with little; the fertile lands are reserved for the sugarcane empire. They have no access to medical services and suffer from malnutrition. Politicians claim to speak on behalf of the people but

their promises to improve their lives are lies. The government ignored them and they are even betrayed by their own humble town brethren. The sad truth is that many claim to be Catholics and want to have their misdeeds blessed by the Church. The rural poor are victims of injustice and greed.[31]

Grande ended his "pastoral letter" with the uplifting thought: "On Sunday the 14th, the Feast of the Resurrection, we will have a popular celebration: They will come with their music from the nearby hamlets, with joy… and some toys and much folklore."[32] He signs off with a final request: "Do not forget to prepare the program for La Cabaña. On Sunday afternoon: do not forget the children's confessions. I will take my time to prepare the homily of Monday 15, at 8 a.m."[33]

Father Rutilio's love for the rural poor inspired his commitment to pursue creative modes for proclaiming the Gospel. From his earliest years of Jesuit formation in Oña, Spain, he found ways to not only catechize the young but also to identify the leadership abilities of those who participated. His time in the seminary of San José de La Montaña as teacher and Prefect of Discipline opened new avenues for ministerial development as he involved the students in the realities of the people that they would eventually serve as priests.

Grande's use of the See-Judge-Act method was coherent with a new approach to ministry that was being used across Latin America. His studies in Belgium at Lumen Vitae, in Quito at IPLA and in other parts of Latin America exposed him to different perspectives that enhanced his intuitive grasp of how to minister. While his studies abroad were rich learning moments, he maintained a special interest and dedication to the people of El Salvador and in particular to the rural poor.

The "pastoral letter" from the roadside is an inspiring expression of such love. Other correspondence provides further understanding of his ministerial concerns and approaches. On 25 August 1970, Rutilio wrote to Father Romeo Maeda to ask that attention be given to a group of older men who were organized for weekly, nightly Adoration of the Eucharist. As Grande explained, for some time, he had been going once per week to El Paisnal to offer some pastoral support. In the process, he witnessed not only the fidelity of these men to the Adoration of the Eucharist, but also the potential they had for becoming involved in evangelization and in the formation of a co-op.

> ... I want to turn them into Leaders for Evangelization, and to this end I have begun to bring three Sisters to found a School of Catechists, which will be attended by two delegates from each hamlet (cantoncito), plus those from the town itself. I have also been speaking to the Worshipers to form a Cooperative as soon as possible, and here my request arises ... I would very much wish that you would provide technical assistance to formalize a cooperative with them.[34]

The approach to rural ministry that Grande was developing caught the attention of colleagues not only within El Salvador, but also beyond its borders. He forged friendships at the IPLA program in Quito and maintained correspondence with them after he returned to El Salvador in the early '70s. Sister Pepa Dominquez wrote him to inquire: "I would like to know if you were finally able to work in the rural areas or with the poor, as you wanted. What lessons did you get out of the stay with Monseñor Proaño...?"[35] Another friend from IPLA wrote to share the outcome of a gathering of "Iplistas" hosted in Mexico. Rodrigo makes special mention of the attendance of Sister María de Jesús from Yakima, Washington. She shared the work that was being done at the grassroots level in Hispanic ministry in the United States. She was personally involved in ministerial rural work in the United States, and shared that at IPLA.[36]

In a Christmas greeting, Alfonso Lopez Trujillo, Secretary General of CELAM expressed his interest in Rutilio's work: "I follow with great joy your work and what you are doing to awaken enthusiasm."[37] Segundo Galilea, a professor of liberation theology in the IPLA program, responded to a letter from Rutilio, expressing his pleasure at hearing that his former student continued his commitment in rural ministry.[38]

The Society of Jesus was also closely following Rutilio's work at Aguilares. César Jerez, Jesuit Provincial, requested a report on the experience of ministry in the parish of Our Lord of Mercies from Octavio Cruz, a diocesan priest and former seminary student of Father Rutilio. Cruz was the only diocesan priest to be integrated into the team ministry that was being carried out in Aguilares. As Cruz reported to Jerez: "At the pastoral level of the diocese, it seems to me that the experience of Aguilares has been a serious attempt to create a new pastoral ministry that responds to the demands and needs of our time."[39] The two goals of the Aguilares effort were clearly articulated by Cruz to Jerez—"to create a living church that is realized and lived in each one of the Christian communities of the parish; the other, to form Christians who are aware of their commitment to integrate the transforming task of our society from the perspective of the necessary historical mediations of God's Kingdom."[40] At length, Cruz outlined the merits and challenges of each goal.

One of the greatest areas of tension was how to integrate a process of evangelization with active engagement in social justice efforts, e.g., building of houses, schools, repairs of streets, collaborative undertakings etc. At the same time, other church ministers felt that the Gospel called them to work toward justice through membership in organizations that opposed political abuse. In the experience of Aguilares, these efforts were sometimes disconnected from each other, that is, the Gospel relevance did not always accompany the parishioners' activism. In spite of the challenges, Cruz expressed hope that in time and with guidance, the rural ministry project of Aguilares would flourish.

Overall, Grande's correspondence that referred to his ministerial efforts is instructive and informative. In a similar fashion, letters written to Grande about his engagement in rural ministry also provide insights into his own ministerial concerns and methods. While ministry was an art form he pursued with passion, intelligence, and dedication, it also was a source of suffering. Sometimes the innovations that this progressive priest implemented were not well received by others who felt more comfortable with the status quo.

Rutilio's approach to seminary formation is an early example of tensions with the hierarchy. Some of the bishops preferred a formation that followed the traditional approach and saw the outreach to the outer communities as negative. Eventually Rutilio's method of formation led to his dismissal from the seminary.

Father Grande's removal from a ministry that he loved and valued affected his relationship with the bishops. He felt the loss of their friendship and confidence. Subsequently while studying at IPLA in Quito, Ecuador, he corresponded with some of the bishops in an effort to heal any ill-feeling. Among those with whom he corresponded were two Salvadorans: Bishop Benjamin Barrera of Santa Ana, and Auxiliary Bishop Óscar Romero of San Salvador.

In a letter written from Quito, Ecuador to Bishop Barrera on 10 July 1972, Rutilio expressed his continued appreciation of their friendship.

> You can be assured, dear Monseñor, that neither distance nor events have erased those pleasant memories. And if some smoke curtains have risen between us, you can be perfectly assured that they are nothing more than that, 'smoke curtains': For my part, at no time have I thought of doubting your kindness and your good intentions.[41]

Grande noted that he passionately loved the Church as others did, but that sometimes it was possible to offend even like-minded persons. But, "a humble and sincere dialogue is undoubtedly the indispensable means that will help us in this common commitment and solidarity."[42]

Bishop Barrera's response expressed his mutual regard and affection dispelling any worry about their personal friendship. In Grande's absence, Barrera reported, the seminary was being led in a different direction; but even that could strengthen the bonds of friendship:

> If there are curtains of smoke, they have to disappear, because the smoke is smoke, and it does not have to resist the force of the true friendship that is strengthened by these tests ... Friends are not hidden from each other by the storm that rages in the soul, as a necessary relief of the human

heart.⁴³

Prior to his return to San Salvador from IPLA, Father Rutilio had also written to Bishop Óscar Romero. He wrote to Romero on the anniversary of his episcopal ordination as auxiliary of San Salvador to dispel any resentment between the two of them. To do so, Grande evoked the fond memory of that occasion as recalled by Romero's words:

> Your letter has made me think a lot; what a coincidence, that on this same day I had a reunion in the Basilica where the altar of that unforgettable concelebration took place...and I have remembered with renewed sentiments of gratitude and affection all the kindnesses, activities and sacrifices that you assumed along with the good lay friends to bring about that unforgettable liturgy in which you were its heart and soul.⁴⁴

After Grande's dismissal from the seminary, Bishop Romero had been placed in charge. It can be surmised from Romero's letter that Rutilio had previously written about his dismissal from the seminary and its present leadership. Some tension between them might be expected, but Romero's further words indicated that Rutilio's letter had eased his fears:

> A thousand thanks for being certain of my right and good intentions and above all of our mutual deep love for the Church. Why is it necessary, in this sincere love of the Church, to have to hurt the heart of the people we most appreciate? Is it a painful part of the passion of the Mystical Body?⁴⁵

Grande's Communication with Political Figures

Several letters between Rutilio Grande and the Mayor of Aguilares as well as the President of the Republic of El Salvador disclose Grande's pastoral communication with political figures. In all of this correspondence, Rutilio, as pastor of Aguilares, strongly clarified for both the Mayor and the President that his role was as the spiritual leader of the parish of Our Lord of Mercies in Aguilares. In a 1973 New Year's letter to José Arñulfo Artiga, Mayor of Aguilares, Father Rutilio took the opportunity to not only extend his best wishes for the New Year, but also to reiterate his pastoral role in the community.

> Faithful to the Lord's command, we want to serve the community of Aguilares, according to the Lord's mandate: 'Go into the world and proclaim my Gospel to all peoples.' Announcing the GOSPEL is our MISSION, nothing else. We are not moved by other interests but those of JESUS CHRIST.[46]

Furthermore, Grande emphasized that a good relationship between the mayor and the parish leaders would be realized as long as both parties... "strive to build a community in which men meet to seek together the common good, without petty interests of individuals or groups: That our only interests be that justice, true fraternity, mutual respect residing within a healthy plurality of opinions."[47]

Throughout his time as pastor of Aguilares, Grande maintained this position always drawing a line between his spiritual leadership and politics. At the same time, his understanding of what it meant to proclaim the Gospel was to uphold the dignity of each person, which required working for justice especially for the poor. When the Interim Mayor of El Paisnal, Adán Roquillo invited Father Grande to attend a reception held in honor of Coronel Arturo Armando Molina, President of the Republic of El Salvador, Rutilio Grande wrote a lengthy letter explaining his reasons for declining the invitation.

> Our people are quite divided by the politics of parties misunderstood and worse practiced. Democracy is merely nominal and the pernicious effects of the last electoral contest still float in the air with their school of resentment at the level of individuals and families.[48]

In 1968, Grande had accepted a similar invitation to attend the installation of a new mayor in El Paisnal. The celebration of Mass by Grande on that occasion had led to major misunderstandings among the people and even resulted in the posting of a protest sign at the entrance of the church. The invitation to

Molina's reception was similar, and Grande declined to attend.

Nevertheless, in the following years of 1973, 1974, 1975, and 1976 Grande received similar invitations for a variety of events that he had to weigh carefully. On one occasion, as noted in a letter of 30 May 1973, Father Rutilio cited the Constitution of El Salvador (Article 25) as a reason for declining attendance at Molina's reception:

> Faithful to my priestly mission that extends to the whole parish community, sincerely attached to the spirit of article 25 of our Political Constitution and in a country like ours where there is separation between Church and State, I want to adjust to the following norms of action, in order to avoid as much ambiguity as possible.[49]

Grande outlined the norms he would follow:

> Not to celebrate religious acts nor to take part in those that are celebrated on the occasion of the installation of Mayors or political authorities ... In general not to take part in acts susceptible to be interpreted as activities of political partisanship.[50]

On the first day of the following year (1974), Grande wrote to Mayor Artiga, greeting him and trying to ease a disagreement that had surfaced between them. What occasioned the tension between the mayor and Grande is not evident. However, while Rutilio's words admonished an unspecified behavior of the mayor, he handled it with finesse. He reiterated that as pastor it was his obligation to point out the wrong committed while continuing to love the person. Father Grande concluded his short message with: "So, know that in many things we will not agree with you, as long as there is no amendment, and I am openly telling you this because I esteem you and I value the whole community even more."[51]

In other instances, Grande received special requests for the celebration of a mass. Some of them, however, had the potential to cause tension. On one occasion, for instance, the Mayor of the Municipality of Aguilares, Rafael Molina Peña, asked that an anniversary Mass be offered for fallen soldiers in the 100-hour war with the neighboring Republic of Honduras that had occurred in 1969. Molina Peña indicated that members of the Armed Forces, of the Democratic National Organization (ORDEN) and others from the community would be present. Prudently and adroitly, Rutilio Grande responded that a public Mass for all the deceased had already been programmed and that they were welcomed to join them in the celebration.[52] Handling the request in this manner, Grande avoided the assumption that those in power could elicit special favors from the clergy. This specific situation could easily have led to a perception that the church was aligning itself with political factions.

While other exchanges with political figures were of a more social nature, Rutilio Grande faced a serious situation as contained in a letter to Rafael Molina Peña, Municipal Mayor of Aguilares (9 February 1976). Father Rutilio had been informed by the mother of a young man named Rigoberto Galvez that a group of men from El Paisnal had been imprisoned the day before. While as yet uninformed of the nature and validity of the charges, Father Rutilio quickly wrote to Molina Peña to forestall any escalation of violence. He called for calm:

> I do not have the slightest doubt that political affairs of parties are involved in this fact, to which I consider myself completely alien; but with this my mediation before you and the security bodies, I want to avoid that the spirits get carried away and we have later to regret the consequences.[53]

Clearly, Father Rutilio Grande as pastoral leader was intimately involved in the many facets of his parishioners' lives, and committed to the announcement of a Gospel that embraced the concerns of the whole person. He neither shied away from speaking against abuses of power nor avoided addressing situations that could compromise the integrity of his pastoral leadership.

Tensions in the Country

As economic and social disintegration in El Salvador created a dire situation of agitation, political tensions grew. For the first time the country suffered a regional trade deficit, and its general foreign trade diminished precipitously. Every day brought news of kidnappings, extortion, murders, and expulsions from the country. As overall discontent grew, the ruling powers ascribed the negative situation to an insidious threat of communist infiltration.[54] Anyone organizing the common people became the targets of repression. That included priests, religious, catechists, delegates of the Word, and active Christians. The following year, the expulsion of foreign church workers escalated. Foreign priests were early targets of this persecution.

As previously discussed, Colombian Father Mario Bernal, pastor in the town of Apopa, was in January 1977 kidnapped, tortured, and then expelled from El Salvador.[55] The Aguilares pastoral team consisted of several priests from outside of El Salvador. Grande became increasingly concerned for their safety. On 22 February 1977, he communicated his anxiety to Bishop Arturo Rivera y Damas. The initial reason for the letter was in response to the preparation of a pastoral triduum that Rivera y Damas had requested of Grande. In his letter, Father Rutilio gave the bishop an overview of his current circumstances:

> Also I must add that I am alone in the parish. Father Benigno Fernández left for Spain last Saturday 19, because of his mother's grave illness. At the request of the Provincial Father, the other priests left yesterday, for a while, due to the insecurity in which the foreign priests are currently experiencing.[56]

He updated Rivera y Damas on the news that Father Barahona of Tecoluca had been imprisoned. At that point, Grande was stretched to the limit, and did not feel that it was prudent to accept the bishop's request.[57] A few weeks later (8 March 1977), Rutilio wrote to Benigno to express every good wish for his mother's recovery. He also described the escalation of tensions.

> Things around here are not going well. It was decreed 'state of siege' on Monday, February 28 in the afternoon throughout the national territory. Opponents, after hearing the verdict of the result of the elections, descended in large number on the park or plaza of La Libertad from February

20 onwards...camping there in the evenings and holding great demonstrations.[58]

With force and tear gas, the army had descended on the protestors driving them to seek refuge in the Church of the Rosary. Archbishop Chávez y González and Bishop Rivera y Damas were summoned on the early morning of February 28 to mediate for the safe release of the people.

Grande continued to report the growing violence inflicted upon those who were protesting the fraudulent presidential election, and the number of priests who had been detained and mistreated. Father Rutilio advised his friend not to return to the country because since the "manifestation of faith" at Apopa protesting Father Mario's torture and exile, Benigno had been placed on a hit list.[59]

In that spiraling situation of terror and violence, Grande was alone. Despite all of this, he found presence of mind to mention his anticipation of the patronal feast of El Paisnal, and Holy Week.[60] Following the penning of that letter, four days later on 12 March 1977, driving the country road to El Paisnal for the celebration of the novena of St. Joseph, patron of his hometown, Father Rutilio Grande was ambushed and assassinated.

Family Correspondence

Through his older brother Flavio, Rutilio Grande maintained regular connection with his family and townspeople of El Paisnal. The full collection of letters that the brothers wrote to each other for almost four decades was, unfortunately, lost. Rutilio, however, kept copies of some of the letters in his personal files. They provide some insight into what the brothers shared with each other and with the extended family.

One of the earliest preserved letters was written on the occasion of the death of Rutilio's brother Salvador who died in Honduras on 1 October 1954 in a car accident while there to work in the fields. A month later, Flavio wrote to explain at length the circumstances of their brother's death, and how comforting it was to know that the people from the town where Salvador lived attended to him with great kindness:

> They tell me that his death was very much felt by that solicitous neighborhood, which attended to him even in his last moments, even when he was totally delivered to the dream of eternity and before the will of God.[61]

A few months later, Rutilio wrote a letter from Oña, Spain to his brothers and family members. In detail he described both the daily schedule followed in the seminary and the direction of his studies in philosophy, cosmology, and psychology. As it was the year of his 27th birthday, he made it a point to mention how so many of his friends had sent him birthday greetings, but that he had not heard from Flavio or other family members. Aside from chiding Flavio for this personal negligence, he asked the following: "When you answer please tell me how the grandmothers (*abuelitas*) are to whom I send my greetings with special affection and I always entrust them especially so that the Lord will grant them what they need most."[62]

During the years of his life outside of El Salvador, he often remembered the "*abuelitas*," the people of El Paisnal and his family. In many ways, the letters written to Flavio were a way of including all of them on his vocational journey. As he prepared for ordination, he told them of the many preparations that were underway. Before ordination he and his thirty-two fellow priestly candidates had taken exams and were going away for some rest followed by eight days of the Spiritual exercises.

Since his family was unable to be present at his ordination in Spain, Rutilio assured them that

> the Consult of El Salvador in Burgos and his wife will be the godparents of my Ordination and of my First Mass...My first Mass will be sung...The bishop will be present at my first Mass, along with all the local community and all their family members and those attending the ordination... The Guerricagoitias from Bilboa will be coming with their two sons.[63]

The Guerricagoitias' son had been a classmate of Rutilio at Oña, but had decided not to be ordained. Nevertheless, the family maintained an intimate relationship with Grande long after his ordination. In the absence of his own family, the Guerricagoitias became Rutilio's extended family and even served as "godparents" for him at the ordination, and are mentioned in the letters that were saved in his files. The family accompanied him throughout the days leading up to his priestly ordination and in the celebrations that followed. During those stages of preparation, Rutilio continued to share events with his older brother. By way of Flavio, Grande sent holy cards marking the ordination to his friends and family members. With his brother he shared his great desire: "That you entrust me very much to the Lord, which is the most important, so that the Priesthood will really transform me into another Christ."[64]

A week after his ordination, Father Rutilio penned a lengthy letter to the entire Grande family. Filled with fervor and emotion he wrote:

> With my hands newly consecrated by the holy anointing I am going to give each and every one of you my PRIESTLY blessing. Kneel and with that I send you [my blessing] filled with affection and with grateful memories: MAY THE BLESSING OF GOD OMNIPOTENT, FATHER, SON AND HOLY SPIRIT, DESCEND ABOUT YOU AND STAY FOREVER. AMEN.[65]

With an outpouring of feeling, he shared with them the personal significance of his ordination.

> On that solemn day, the great powers of JESUS CHRIST were granted me by the Bishop and from that time on I became another Christ to forgive the sins of men, to administer the Sacraments of His Church, to evangelize men, to celebrate the Holy Sacrifice by miraculously descending into my hands his BODY and his HOLY BLOOD ...[66]

The newly ordained priest was overwhelmed with poignant remembrance of his childhood desires:

> You cannot imagine the state of my soul in those happy moments. It was a feeling of the close embrace of CHRIST, an intimate embrace, which I have awaited for so many years. From that sacred

summit of the PRIESTHOOD I have seen in an instant and from a bird's eye view all the years since I, as a child, had desired to be a PRIEST.[67]

Because his family was unable to be in Spain with him, he shared the many details of the celebration of his first Mass and the reception that followed. So they might be with him despite the geographical distance, he asked them to have a Mass celebrated in El Paisnal on the day of his ordination. Rutilio assured his family that he had remembered them all as he celebrated his first Mass. "Your names were passing through my mind. Moments of silent weeping, filled with distant memories, full of names and events, a look at my little land and my little village far away ..."[68]

Grande loved his family but had special affection for the women who raised him. His paternal grandmother Francisca and his sister-in-law Lolita Grande Pineda shaped much of his childhood. The death of Francisca in 1963 was a great loss for him. In April of that year, Rutilio answered a letter from Flavio that had informed him of his beloved grandmother's passing:

> She, the one who prepared the food for a long time. When we sat at the table with our father to eat from the same dish in our solitary home, and the one who prepared the food that I carried and took to the 'boys' as she used to say...She who taught me so many good things.[69]

Although at a distance, he kept informed on what was happening in El Salvador and even in his small hometown of El Paisnal. In some ways, he maintained oversight of what was pastorally occurring in the town of his birth. In certain instances, he was involved in the selection of priests assigned to attend its people.

While his initial studies were in Oña, Spain, in the early '60s, he also spent time in France to study the language. He took advantage of his stay there, to visit the many tourist sites like Notre Dame, the Eiffel Tower, the Arc de Triomphe, and Versailles, each of which he described in his letters to Flavio. Following his study of the French language, he traveled to Lumen Vitae in Brussels to be educated in the latest catechetical methods.

Lumen Vitae, in both its publications and in its teaching, focused on the formation of students in the fields of Pastoral Theology and Catechesis. The program employed a three-pronged methodology: the analysis of cultural contexts, theological reflection on the results of analysis, and the acquisition of skills and knowledge for designing Catechetical and Pastoral projects. Critical to this exploration were issues of global context, cultural exchange, interreligious dialogue, ethics, justice, democracy and personal development.

From his early Jesuit formation in Oña, Spain, Rutilio had an intuitive interest in catechetics. The spirit generated by the Second Vatican Council positioned Lumen Vitae as a meeting place for international exchange among pastoralists from Africa, Asia, Latin America, and North America.[70] Providentially, Rutilio found himself at the center of this rich, exciting pastoral and theological dynamic. Always maintaining the bond with his family, letters to and from Flavio earmarked all these varied locations.

In many letters, Rutilio shared details of his life and made comments both serious and humorous:

> I feel a little tired. We're getting old. My hair is getting more and more white; but all this is nothing, absolutely nothing compared to the cross that the Lord has wanted to put on the shoulders of our brother Alberto.... A greeting to each and every one, not forgetting the nephews and none of our friends.[71]

Characteristically his concerns turned to others. His brother Alberto's health and decline was the subject in several of his letters. At the same time, to Flavio he acknowledged the fatigue of his busy days but dismissed it as part of that aging process from which neither of them were exempted.

His domestic letters reveal him as a man sensitive to the need for human warmth and love. On a number of occasions, he expressed his hurt to Flavio.

> It appears that you do not want anything to do with me anymore. It has been a long time since I received news from you and I still do not know whether or not you have received my letter from

> the end of December. I am in charge of distributing the correspondence here and every day when they deliver the batch of letters, I take a look to see if there is something from my homeland and from my own; but I have been disillusioned for some time. It is true that I am a religious and that I have renounced many things for the love of God. So that is true. But I have not renounced the love of my homeland or my own, on the contrary I love them immensely through God.[72]

Although it is clear that he wrote this letter from the College Novitiate of San Francisco de Borja in Córdoba, Spain, it is not dated. Nevertheless, it is easy to conjure up an image of Rutilio as a young aspiring Jesuit in formation far away from his homeland and his own family, a challenging situation in many ways. The letter, however, touchingly reveals his very tender need for human affection.

A few days before Christmas 1971 when Grande was in Nicaragua, he wrote to Flavio and the family to describe his new surroundings. As he often did, Rutilio pictured the city of Managua with its surrounding lakes and volcanoes. Grande was struck by the natural phenomenon of sharks in Lake Cocibolca in Granada, Nicaragua. "It is the only lake in the world that has sharks, as they are sea animals, which means that this lake, at one time, was connected to the sea."[73] He lamented that given the political tensions between El Salvador and Honduras, to avoid trespassing on Honduran territory, he had not been able to travel by bus. He felt that geographical boundaries that separated many of the Central American countries were unfortunate. "So it is the fate of these small nations that should have been united long ago forming a great nation, Central America."[74]

Although Grande was following developments in the electoral process in El Salvador, Nicaragua did not have extended media coverage of what was happening in his own country. He asked his brother Flavio to send him newspaper clippings. His interest in the political life of El Salvador had awakened in him the idea of writing articles for the local newspaper, *La Prensa Gráfica*.[75] In due time, he became a valued contributor to El Salvador's local newspapers.

Father Grande kept informed on the political life of not only El Salvador, but also of the other Latin American countries. Even while he visited the Guarani Indians in the highlands surrounding Panama, he followed the news. "Precisely, on the mountain, with the Indians, I learned yesterday, on the radio, that President Velasco Ibarra has been deposed in Ecuador in a military coup. They put him in a plane and sent him to Panama. Yesterday he left for Argentina."[76]

Perspective

Over the many years of his life, Rutilio Grande engaged in revealing communication with a wide range of people: his family, friends, Jesuit colleagues, lay ministers, clergy and religious and members of the church hierarchy. Because he took care to maintain this correspondence in his personal files, he left a legacy of letters that serve to preserve a poignant portrait of the man. In particular, he treasured the letters exchanged with his beloved spiritual father, friend and mentor, Archbishop Chávez y González. In those letters, he frequently recalled his childhood desire to become a priest, and he shared many dimensions of his life journey. Others of his letters reference his chronic health problems and disclose how he faced them with quiet acceptance. Although he seldom shared his illness with others—even his family—in a few exchanges he had with Jesuit superiors he shares his determined handling of that personal challenge. His concerns about ministry frequently feature in his correspondence, highlighting his passion to develop methods to effectively transmit the Gospel message. Grande's friends were very much aware of his zeal in ministry, conversing about it in several exchanges of letters with him.

A man keenly committed to the transformation of society for the benefit of all God's people, especially the poor, Grande kept himself informed on the social realities of the time, and he reflected on that complex reality through the lens of the Gospel. In spite of the pull of his many obligations and involvements, Rutilio maintained warm communication with those he loved, especially his family and the people of his cherished hometown of El Paisnal. For us, his letters, besides presenting his interests, concerns, and challenges, also discloses the rich humanity of Rutilio Grande.

NOTES

1. Letter from Rutilio Grande to Archbishop Luis Chávez y González dated 11 January 1976 (APCSJ). Spanish citation: Desde entonces guardo archivadas sus muchas cartas, como un testimonio que comprueba lo que le digo, pues siempre me he comunicado con Usted lo largo de las diversas etapas de mi vida: como niño desde mi pueblo, a raíz de su primera Visita Pastoral, como Seminarista a traves de mis cinco años de Seminario, y en los diversos periodos de mi formación en la Compañia de Jesús, a la que ingrese con su benevola aquiescencia.
2. Letter from Archbishop Luis Chávez y González dated 12 May 1940 (APCSJ). Spanish citation: En este día que te escribo Celebramos el DIA PRO SEMINARIO, día grande por ser la festividad de PENTECOSTES, día en el cual la Iglesia conmemora la VENIDA DEL ESPIRITU SANTO, por lo cual te suplico encarecidamente que le pidas mucho al Espíritu Santo, que es Dios como el Padre y el Hijo, que si es de su agrado que se realicen tus santos deseos de ser SACERDOTE.
3. Letter from Archbishop Luis Chávez y González dated 21 July 1949 (APCSJ) . Spanish citation: A mi regreso de la Ciudad Eterna, Roma, encontré tu atenta carta, por la que me felicitas con ocasión del día de mi Santo Patrono, San Luis. Dios Nuestro Señor te pagará tu santos recuerdos, y muy especialmente el Ramillete. The word "Ramillete" refers to a popular practice of the time to offer a "bouquet" made up of prayers, attendance at Mass(es), small expression of penances on behalf of person being honored.
4. Letter from Archbishop Luis Chávez y González dated 18 July 1958 (APCSJ). Spanish citation: Con un afectuoso y cariñoso saludo te envío esta carta en la víspera de tu ordenación sacerdotal; con ella van mis oraciones particulares para que Dios Nuestro Señor y la Sma. Virgen María te guarden y protejan en tu sacerdocio, pues sin la gracia de dios y la asistencia de la Sma. Madre, poco podremos hacer en tan sublima é incomparable estado, el SACERDOCIO.
5. Letter from Archbishop Chávez y González to Rutilio Grande dated 28 September 1962 (APCSJ). Spanish citation: En tus oraciones te ruego pidas muchísimo por los sacerdotes, para que vivan en gracia de Dios y asi estar animados del "alma de verdadero apostolado.
6. Letter from Archbishop Chávez y González to Rutilio Grande dated 3 September 1963 (APCSJ). Spanish citation: ...debes estar completamente tranquilo, pues actualmente tiene a su cargo la Parroquia el Padre José C. Pineda y él tiene especiales instrucciones de atender El Paisnal, ademas los seminaristas continuan dando el catesismo.
7. Letter from Chávez y González to Rutilio Grande dated 8 June 1964 (APCSJ). Spanish citation: ...los días 18-19 del corriente estare en tu pueblo, El Paisnal, recordando tus años de niñez. ... (18-19 days of this month I will be in your town, El Paisnal, remembering your years of childhood.)
8. Letter from Archbishop Chávez y González to Rutilio Grande dated 3 August 1972 (APCSJ).
9. Contract between the Diocese of San Salvador and the Jesuits of Central America dated 7 November 1975 (APCSJ). Team members: Jesuits Rutilio Grande, Benigno Fernández, Salvador Carranza and diocesan priest Octavio Cruz.
10. Letter from Archbishop Chávez y González to Rutilio Grande dated 17 December 1974 (APCSJ). Spanish citation: "Después de Dios, a Usted le debo mi vocación como instrumento visible de la gracia del Señor: Por medio de Usted quiso llamarme explícitamente Aquel que me había escogido para esta vocación de servicio en Su Iglesia."
11. Letter from Rutilio Grande to Archbishop Chávez y González dated 11 January 1976 (APCSJ). Spanish citation: Lo que le voy a manifestar no es el fruto de una decisión veleidosa o inmadura, sino el fruto de una larga reflexión, profundizada primeramente en mís ocho días

de Ejercicios Espirituales hechos en soledad...y luego continuada en el transcurso de estos meses pasados."
12. Ibid. Spanish citation: Hay que tener en cuenta que por tratarse de jóvenes, algunos de ellos se comportan en sus acciones dentro del marco evolutivo propio de su edad. Es posible que nosotros los adultos pequemos por otros extremos. Lo cierto es que a mi personalment me han ayudado en un proceso de conciencia y de conversión, sin que esto quiera decir que acepte todas las posturas de algunos de ellos sin la debida reserva.
13. Ibid. Por mi parte, me pondré en manos de mis superiores para que dispongan de mí. Es posible que en cualquier otra parte más necesitada pueda prestar mi servicio al Señor, en algún sitio de C.A.
14. Letter from Rutilio Grande to Jesuit Vice-Provincial (no personal name included) dated 8 July 1954 (APCSJ). Spanish citation: Gracias a Dios, voy de mejor a mejor. Esta gordura que he conseguido a raíz de lo de Panamá, me ayuda, según lo voy experimentando, para todo. Espero qu se consolidará y que no pasará los justos limites. Según recuerdo, le dije a V.R. que todo esto de inspecciones, clases, trato con los Seminaristas, me ayuda mucho aún para la salud, como lo he notado desde que pasé de Sta. Tecla al Seminario.
15. Letter from Rutilio Grande to Agustín Bariáin, Jesuit Vice-Provincial dated 4 December 1955 (APCSJ). Spanish citation: Fuí a Bilbao para examen con el Dr. Gonzalez Pinto (buen Psiquiatra) quién después de examinarme largamente durante una hora y cuarto, me dijo que podía estar completamente tranquilo. Eso mismo decía yo en mi interior desde ya hacía tiempo... Corporalmente, gracias a Dios, estoy muy sano y fuerte. No me pierdo un paseo de campo o una matinal, ya que esos trotes por los montes me descansan enormemente y me dejan como nuevo para enfrentarme con la semana siguiente. Hago gimasia metódica diariamente durante un cuarto de hora al levantarme y me va muy bien. Duermo por ahora únicamente lo que la comunidad permite y ciertamente con fruto. Al frío cada día lo voy considerando más como un benefactor: me ha robustecido, es un estimulante maravilloso del apetito, etc. O sea que en todo esto, bien, como puede ver. Todos los días lo pido al Señor con especial empeño el don de una buena salud y creo que de mi parte también pongo los medios.
16. Letter from Rutilio to Miguel Elizondo, Jesuit Vice-Provincial dated 9 April 1956 (APCSJ). Spanish citation: Aparentemente estoy con muy buena salud y robusto físicamente. Con todo, el sistema nervioso lo tengo siempre débil. Es mi cruz. Con esto cuento, pero confío perfectamente que triunfaré, con la ayuda de Dios, de todas las dificultades. Es admirable el optimismo que Dios me concede. Muchas veces pedí en el Noviciado una cruz fuerte y pesada, y nunca me imaginé que esta iba a ser mi cruz. La he abrazado desde hace mucho tiempo con todas sus consecuencias...
17. Ibid. Spanish citation: Además todo el mundo cree que ya me encuentro perfectamente, me ven robusto y con salud fisica externa y yo me guardo muy bien de quejarme y desahogarme va no sea con los que me dirigen.
18. See: Ana María Pineda, *Romero & Grande: Companions on the Journey*, 70.
19. Letter from Grande to Provincial Segundo Azcue dated 14 July 1968 (APCSJ). Spanish citation: Parece que nos falta el "elán apostólico-pastoral" en nuestras obras, elán que nace de una visión pastoral y de un actuar conforme a esta visión. En ese ambiente se movían nuestros primeros Padres, aquel grupo de San Ignacio y sus compañeros...Ese dinamismo tenía todo aquel equipo, en ese ambiente se movía, eso revisaban en común de eso hablaban, era su vida...Parece que ese debiera ser siempre el espirítu que deberia existir en nuestras comunidades.
20. Ibid. Spanish citation: ...con no mucha proyección hacia el mundo circundante, como aislados de las tremendas realidades que los rodean, realidades sociales, morales y religiosas.
21. Letter from Rutilio Grande to Jesuit Provincial (no name included), 30 November 1969 (APCSJ). While Grande addressed the recipient of the letter by title but not name, it can be presumed that it is Segundo Azcue.
22. Letter from Rutilio Grande to Flavio Grande, 19 February 1972 (APCSJ). Spanish citation: Son gente abandonada de todos: de la Iglesia y de la gente de gobierno. Allá no sube nadie ni

siquiera el sacerdote. Y la gente está sin bautizar, ya mayores! Hacía 15 años había subido un Obispo y desde entonces no había subido un sacerdote.

23. Ibid. Spanish citation: Encantado me quedaría en medio de aquellos pobres indios, trabajando toda la vida, a fin de levantarlos en todo sentido.

24. Letter from Rutilio Grande to Jesuit Provincial Francisco Estrada, only year of 1972 is noted (APCSJ). Spanish citation: Si no tienes dificultad, a mi me interesaría quedarme después de terminado el IPLA, unos quince días en Riobamba para profundizar más en un asunto de suma importancia, como es ése...[también] desearía detenerme nuevamente en Panamá para ver con detenimiento algunas experiencias a la luz del curso IPLA.

25. Letter from Rutilio Grande to Francisco Estrada, SJ, 26 February 1972 (APCSJ). Spanish citation: Le hablé con sinceridad a Sosa acerca de que tiene que cambiar totalmente de método, es decir, la misita, los bautizos, y pasar a dividir en zonas la población para ir estableciendo células de familias, con reuniones diarias por la noche en casas particulares, captando líderes seglares, en un plan de acercamiento y de evangelización progresiva. De lo contrario no vale la pena estar ahí...

26. Letter from Rutilio Grande to Francisco Estrada, SJ, 24 September 1975 (APCSJ). Spanish citation: Es hermoso constatar cómo en todas partes de nuestros cinco naciones de C.A. y Panamá, se están haciendo laudables esfuerzos en nuestra Iglesia para anunciar fielmente el Evangelio a los diferentes grupos humanos de nuestras Repúblicas. Es el Evangelio de Jesús y su fuerza dinamizadora (transformadora) la que está cambiando el rostro de nuestra Iglesia. Les animo con toda la convicción personal, a que sigamos trabajando en todas nuestras comunidades para comprender y tratar de vivir el Evangelio para el bien de nuestros pueblos.

27. Letter from Rutilio Grande to Chávez y González, 26 April 1974 (APCSJ). Spanish citation: También nos interesa la Biblia en Imágenes para niños tanto para el campo como para la ciudad pues tenemos catecismos interrumpidamente durante el año y también en ellos seguimos con la debida metodología los pasos de la biblia.

28. Letter from Rutilio Grande to Julio Lopez de la Puente, S.J., 20 May 1965 (APCSJ).

29. Letter from Rutilio Grande to Jesuit team members at Aguilares, 9 April 1974 (APCSJ). Spanish citation: Les escribo esta carta debajo de un hermoso amate, mientras los tuncos andan por los alrededores, mientras los gallos cantan, y veo las caras pálidas de unos niños con el estómago abultado. Son las 4:30 p.m. y dentro de muy poco tiempo estarán llegando en procesión de diversos caseríos, para la celebración de la Palabra de Dios con estas humildes gentes que son tan hijos de Dios y hermanos nuestros como los de Aguilares y como los hombres de cualquier parte del mundo.

30. Ibid. Spanish citation: Todas estas humildes gentes son las tributarias de Aguilares y del El Paisnal, en lo commercial y en lo politico. Para allá salen en caravana...para trabajar en las llanuras ricas en caña, donde dejan el sudor de su trabajo, su vida y su salud, plara ganar unos pinches centavos, mientras los dueños de tales grandísimas propiedades van colocando sus grandes cantidades de dinero en los bancos de dentro y fuera del país.

31. Ibid.

32. Ibid. Spanish citation: El Domingo 14, de Resurrección, tendremos aquí una fiestecita popular: Vendrán con sus conjuntos de los cantones de los alrededores, con alegría con numerito y algunos juegos y mucho folklore.

33. Ibid. Spanish citation: No olviden prevenir el programa de La Cabaña. El Domingo por la tarde: no olviden las confesiones de los niños de allá. Ya me tomaré mi tiempo para prepara la homilía del día Lunes 15, a las 8 a.m.

34. Letter from Rutilio Grande to Father Romero Maeda, 25 August 1970 (APCSJ). Spanish citation: ...yo quiero convertirlos en Líderes para la Evangelizacion, y con este fin he comenzado a llevar tres Monjitas para fundar un Escuela de Catequistas, a la que acudirán dos delegados de cada cantoncito, más los del propio pueblo. También les he venido hablando a los Adoradores de formar cuanto antes una Cooperativa, y aquí surge mi petición...Yo desearía muy de veras que Ustedes le prestasen asistencia técnica para formalizar con ellos una cooperativa.

35. Letter from Sister Pepa Dominguez to Rutilio Grande, 3 July 1973 (APCSJ). Spanish citation:

Rutilio Grande

Me gustaría saber si pudiste al fin trabajar en el campo o con los pobres, como querías. Que enseñanzas sacaste de la estadía con Monseñor Proaño...

36. Letter to Rutilio Grande from Rodrigo (no surname included), Mexico, D.F., 26 January 1974 (APCSJ)
37. Letter from Alfonso Lopez Trujillo to Rutilio Grande, 22 December 1975 (APCSJ). Spanish citation: Sigo, con mucha alegría sus trabajos y lo que haces allí para despertar entusiasmo.
38. See: *Romero & Grande*, 49.
39. Letter from Jesús Octavio Cruz to César Jerez, 23 August 1976 (APCSJ). Spanish citation: A nivel de la pastoral de la diócesis me parece que la experiencia de Aguilares ha sido un intento serio de creación de una nueva pastoral que responde a las exigencias y necesidades de nuestro tiempo.
40. Ibid. Spanish citation: ...crear una iglesia viva que se realiza y vivencia en cada una de las comunidades cristianas de la parroquia, la otra, la de formar cristianos que consientes de su compromiso se integren a la tarea transformadora de nuestra sociedad desde la perspectiva de las necesarias mediaciones históricas del Reino de Dios.
41. Letter from Rutilio Grande to Bishop Benjamin Barrera, 10 July 1972 (APCSJ). Spanish citation: Puedo asegurarle, querido Monseñor, que ni la distancia ni los acontecimientos han podido borrar esos gratos recuerdos. Y si algunas cortinas de humo se han levantado entre nosotros, puede estar perfectamente seguro de que no son más que esto, "cortinas de humo": Por mi parte, en ningún momento se me ha ocurrido dudar de su bondad y de sus retas intenciones.
42. Ibid. Spanish citation: El diálogo humilde y sincero, es sin duda, el medio imprescindible que nos ayudará en este empeño común y solidario.
43. Ibid. Spanish citation: Si hay cortinas de humo, tienen que desaparecer, porque el humo es humo, y no ha de resistir la fuerza de la amistad verdadera que se viene a fortalecer con estas pruebas...A los amigos no se les oculta la tempestad que bulla en el alma, como un desahogo necesario del corazón humano.
44. Letter from Óscar Romero to Rutilio Grande, 22 June 1972 (APCSJ). Spanish citation: Su carta me ha hecho pensar mucho; que casualidad, que ese mismo día tuve una reunion en la Basílica donde se conserva el altar de aquella involvidable concelebración...y he recordado con nuevos sentimientos de gratitud y cariño todas las finezas, actividades y sacrificios que Ud. se impuso junto con los buenos amigos seglares para lograr aquella inolvidable liturgia en la Ud. fue el alma.
45. Ibid. Mil gracias por estar seguro de mi recta y buena intención y sobre todo de nuestro mutuo y profundo amor a la Iglesia. Porqué será necesario, en este sincero amor a la Iglesia, tener que lastimar el corazón de las personas que más apreciamos? Será una parte dolorosa de la pasión del Cuerpo Místico?
46. Letter from Rutilio Grande to José Arnulfo Artiga, Mayor of Aguilares, 1 January 1973 (APCSJ). Spanish citation: Fieles al mandato del Señor, queremos servir a la comunidad de Aguilares, según el mandato del Señor: "Id por el mundo y anunciad mi Evangelio a todas las gentes." Anunciar el EVANGELIO es nuestra MISION, ni más ni menos. No nos mueven otros intereses sino los de JESUCRISTO.
47. Ibid. Spanish citation: ...todos nos esforcemos por construir una comunidad en la que los hombres se encuentren para busar todos juntos el bien común, sin intereses mezquinos de individuos o de grupos: Que nuestros únicos intereses sean la justicia, la verdadera fraternidad, el respeto mutuo dentro de una sana pluralidad de opinones.
48. Letter from Rutilio Grande to Adán Ronquillo, Interim Mayor of El Paisnal, 24 May 1973 (APCSJ). Spanish citation: Nuestro pueblo está bastante dividido por la política de partidos mal entendida y peor practicada. La democracia es meramente nominal y los afectos pernisciosos de la pasada contienda electoral todavía flotan en el ambiente con su secuela de resentimientos a nivel de personas y de familias.
49. Letter from Rutilio Grande to José Arnulfo Artica, Mayor of Aguilares, 30 May 1973 (APCSJ). Spanish citation: Fiel a mi misión sacerdotal que se extiende a toda la comunidad par-

roquial, apegado sinceramente al espíritu del artículo 25 de nuestra Constitución Política y en un país como el nuestro en donde existe separación entre la Iglesia y el Estado, yo quiero ajustarme a las siguientes normas de acción, a fin de evitar en lo posible toda ambiguedad.

50. Ibid. Spanish citation: No celebrar actos religiosos ni tomar parte en los que se celebren con ocasión de la toma de posesión de Alcaldes o autoridades políticas...En general no tomar parte en actos susceptibles de ser interpretados como actividades de partidismo político.
51. Letter from Rutilio Grande to Jose Arnulfo Artiga, Mayor of Aguilares, 9 January 1974 (APSJ). Spanish citation: Así pues, sepa que en muchas cosas no estaremos de acuerdo con Usted, mientras no haya enmienda, y esto se lo digo paladinamente porque lo estimo a Usted y estimo mucho más todavía a la colectividad entera.
52. Ibid. See letter for context of the request and Grande's response.
53. Letter from Rutilio Grande to Rafael Molina Peña, Municipal Mayor of Aguilares, 9 February 1976 (APCSJ). Spanish citation: No me cabe la menor duda de que en este hecho andan implicados asuntos políticos de partidos, a los cuales me considero ajeno plenamente; pero con esta mi mediación ante Usted y los cuerpos de seguridad, quiero evitar que se vayan caldeando los ánimos y tengamos más adelante que lamentar las consecuencias.
54. See: *Romero & Grande*, 124.
55. Ibid.
56. Letter from Rutilio Grande to Bishop Arturo Rivera Damas, 22 February 1977 (APCSJ). Spanish citation: También debo añadirle que me encuentro sólo en la Parroquia. El Padre Benigno Fernández salió para España el pasado Sábado 19, a causa de la gravedad de su mamá. Por disposición del Padre Provincial, salieron de aquí ayer los otros Padres, durante una temporada, a causa de la inseguridad en que actualmente se encuentran los Sacerdotes extranjeros.
57. Ibid.
58. Letter from Rutilio Grande to Benigno Fernández, SJ, 8 March 1977 (APCSJ). Spanish citation: Las cosas por aquí no muy bien que se diga. Fué decretado "estado de sitio" el lunes 28 de Febrero por la tarde en todo el territorio nacional. Los oposicionistas, una vez oída la sentencia consabida del resultado de las elecciones, se apostaron masivamente en el parque o plaza de La Libertad del 20 de febrero en adelante y cada vez más in crescendo, acampando por las noches allá y en grandes demostraciones. Hasta que el día 27, al filo de la media noche, el ejército los desajojo...
59. Ibid.
60. Ibid.
61. Letter from Flavio Grande to Rutilio Grande, 8 November 1954 (APCSJ). Spanish citation: Me cuentan que su muerte fué muy sentida por aquella vecindad bienhechora, que le prodigó atenciónes hasta en sus últimos instantes, aun cuando vacía entregado al sueño de la eternidad y ante la voluntad de Dios.
62. Letter from Rutilio Grande to Flavio Grande, 24 July 1955 (APCSJ). Spanish citation: Cuando me contestéis contadme por favor cómo se encuentran las abuelitas a quienes saludo con especial cariño y las encomiendo siempre muy especialmente para que el Señor les conceda aquello que más les convenga.
63. Letter from Rutilio Grande to Flavio Grande, 19 June 1959 (APCSJ). Spanish citation: El Señor Consul de El Salvador en Burgos y su señora seran los padrinos de mi Ordenación y de mi Primera Misa...Mi primera Misa sera cantada...Asiste a esa Misa el Señor Obispo, toda la Comunidad y todos los familiars y gente asistente a las Ordenaciones...De Bilbao vendran los Sres. De Guerricagoitia con sus dos hijos...
64. Letter from Rutilio Grande to Flavio Grande, 2 July 1959 (APCSJ). Spanish citation: Que me encomendeis mucho al Señor que es lo más importante a fin de que el Sacerdocio me transforme realmente en otro Cristo.
65. Letter from Rutilio Grande to Familia Grande Garcia, 7 August 1959 (APCSJ). Spanish citation: Con mis manos recién consagradas por la unción santa os voy a dar a todos y cada uno

Rutilio Grande

de vosotros mi bendición de SACERDOTE. Poneos de rodillas y ahí os va plena de cariño y llena de gratísimos recuerdos: LA BENDICION DE DIOS OMNIPOTENTE, PADRE, HIJO Y ESPIRITU SANTO, DECIENDA SOBRE VOSOTROS Y PERMANEZCA PARA SIEMPRE. AMEN.

66. Ibid. Spanish citation: En ese día solemne me fueron concedidos por manos del Señor Obispo los grandes poderes de JESUCRISTO y quede convertido desde entonces en OTRO CRISTO para perdonar en su nombre los pecados de los hombres, para administrar los Sacramentos de su Iglesia, para evangelizar a los hombres, para celebrar el Santo Sacrificio haciendo descender milagrosamente a mis manos su CUERPO y su SANGRE SANTISIMOS...

67. Ibid. Spanish citation: No os podeis imaginar el estado de mi alma en aquellos dichosos momentos. Era un sentir el abrazo estrecho de CRISTO, abrazo íntimo, esperando hacía ya tantos años. Desde esa cumbre sagrada del SACERDOCIO he visto en un instante y a vuelo de pájaro todos los años transcurridos desde que, siendo niño, tuve deseos de ser SACERDOTE.

68. Ibid. Spanish citation: Fueron pasando por mi mente vuestros nombres queridos. Momentos de un llorar silencioso, llenos de recuerdos lejanos, llenos de nombres y de episodios, un mirar hacia mi pequeña tierra y hacia mi pequeño pueblo lejano...

69. Letter from Rutilio Grande to Flavio Grande, 3 April 1963 (APCSJ). Spanish citation: Ella, la que nos preparó la comida durante mucho tiempo. Cuando nos sentábamos a la mesa con nuestro padre para comer de un mismo plato en la casa solariega, y la que preparaba aquellos "bastimentos" que yo trasportaba y llevaba a los "muchachos" como ella solía decir…Ella, la que me enseño a mi tantas cosas buenas.

70. See: *Romero & Grande*, 43.

71. Letter from Rutilio Grande to Flavio Grande, 1 July 1964 (APCSJ). Spanish citation: Me siento un poco cansado. Ya vamos para viejos. Mi pelo se va poniendo cada vez más blanco; pero todo esto es nada, absolutamente nada en comparación con la cruz que el Señor ha querido poner sobre las espaldas de nuestro hermano Alberto....Un saludo a todos y cada uno, sin olvidar a los sobrinos y a ninguno de nuestros amigos.

72. Letter from Rutilio Grande to Flavio Grande, no date noted (APCSJ). Spanish citation: Se ve que ya no quereis nada que ver conmigo. Hace ya mucho tiempo que no recibo noticias vuestras y no sé todavia si habeis recibido o no mi carta de finales de Diciembre. Yo soy encargado de repartir aquí la correspondencia y todos los días cuando me entregan el lote de cartas, echo un vistazo para ver si hay algo de la tierra y de los míos; pero me vengo desilusionando hace ya bastante tiempo! Es verdad que soy religioso y que he renunciado a muchas cosas por amor de Dios. Asi es verdad. Pero no he renunciado al amor a mi tierra y a los míos, al contrario los amo inmensamente através de Dios.

73. Letter from Rutilio Grande to Flavio Grande, 21 December 1971 (APCSJ). Spanish citation: Es el único lago en el mundo que tiene tiburones, ya que son animales propios del mar, lo cual quiere decir que este lago, por lo visto, en un tiempo estuvo comunicado con el mar.

74. Ibid. Spanish citation: Así andamos estos pequeños pedacitos de nación que deberían estar unidos hace mucho tiempo formando una gran nación, Centro America.

75. Ibid.

76. Letter from Rutilio Grande to Flavio Grande, 19 February 1972 (APCSJ). Spanish citation: Precisamente, estando allá en la montaña, con los indios, me enteré el día pasado, por la radio, que el Presidente Velasco Ibarra ha sido depuesto en El Ecuador, en un golpe de estado de los militares. Lo metieron en un avión y lo enviaron a Panamá. Ayer salió para la Argentina.

CHAPTER 4

ROMERO'S SERMONS ON RUTILIO GRANDE

On 4 February 2015, the Vatican announced Pope Francis's decision to beatify Archbishop Óscar Romero. Archbishop Vincenzo Paglia, the Vatican official leading Romero's process of beatification, also announced the initiation of the beatification process for Rutilio Grande, S.J. Subsequently, the Prefect also noted: "It is impossible to know Romero without knowing Rutilio Grande."[1] In doing so, Paglia promoted the common belief that Romero and Grande maintained a very close friendship. Popular devotion for the two martyrs has developed the idea of Grande's death creating a climactic moment of conversion for Romero, but research paints another less dramatic, yet perhaps more humanly inspiring picture of the relationship between the two men.

With the passage of the years, it is difficult to fully ascertain the actual degree of their friendship. Nevertheless, Archbishop Romero's sermons shed light on the significance of Rutilio Grande in Romero's life, as well as in the life of the Church in El Salvador and the nation as a whole.

In eight of his sermons between 1977-80, Romero specifically speaks about Grande. Five of those sermons devote major attention to the memory of his friend. Significantly, three other sermons include further references to Father Grande.

At Rutilio Grande's funeral on 14 March 1977 Romero delivered the first sermon. In his opening words, the Archbishop poignantly presented not only his personal sentiments but also what he considered to be the significance of Grande's life:

> If this were an ordinary funeral, I would speak here, my dear sisters and brothers, about the hu-

man and personal relationship that I shared with Father Rutilio Grande whom I considered a brother. At important moments in my life, he was very close to me and I will never forget his gestures of friendship. But this is not the time to speak about my personal feelings but to proclaim, in the presence of these bodies, a message for all of us who continue the pilgrimage of life.[2]

While personally grieving Grande's murder, the Archbishop chose to help the mourning faithful to understand the deeper meaning in Rutilio's death. Romero's opening question focused on the significance of Grande's life: "What is the role of the Church in this universal struggle for liberation from so much misery?"(Ibid.) He used Paul VI's apostolic exhortation on *Evangelization in the Modern World* (*Evangelii nuntiandi*) as the framework for his sermon. The guidelines in the document create a lens through which the faithful can best understand the martyred priest. Paul VI clearly indicates that the role of the Church is to cry out with those "who remain on the margin of life, famine, chronic disease, illiteracy, poverty." (Ibid. §30) It is the Church's responsibility to be uniquely present in the struggle against injustice, always promoting and respecting human dignity.[3] Both dimensions were eminently embraced and lived by Rutilio Grande.

As Romero continued his funeral sermon he reminded the faithful that Grande had always maintained that his calling was to proclaim the Gospel and not be aligned with any political party. Grande worked diligently toward achieving liberation for the poor from the many injustices they suffered in El Salvador. Yet all his efforts stemmed from the inspiration of faith. Those who knew Rutilio knew this to be true. Furthermore, Romero's words underscored Grande's commitment to justice and dignity:

> My sisters and brothers, let no one here present think that this gathering in the presence of Father Grande's body is some political act with sociological or economic implications. No, it is not that, rather [it] is a gathering in faith—a faith that through Father Grande's body, dead in hope, is opened to eternal horizons.[4]

Grande had embraced the social teaching of the Church fully believing that it was his Christian call to work alongside those entrusted to his pastoral leadership. Together they worked to transform the social constructs that diminished the life of the poor and stood in the way of the attainment of full human dignity. He was assassinated because he lived and preached the social teaching of the Church.

In his sermon, Romero observed that "the Church's social doctrine is often viewed as subversive, and yet this is so far removed from the wisdom of the Church's doctrine which is proposed as a basis for our lives." (Ibid.) As Father Grande's pastoral work in Aguilares demonstrated, he dedicated himself to the poor. In their humble dwellings he ate with them and listened to their needs and aspirations. He helped them to discover their own gifts and inspired them to use their personal skills and talents in creating their own futures.

Archbishop Romero understood that Rutilio's life of accompanying the poor was a precious inheritance, a model for priests to imitate. In the final words of his sermon, Romero referred to Grande's death as that of martyrdom: "Perhaps this is why God chose Father Rutilio for martyrdom because those whom he knew and those who knew him are well aware of the fact that he never called people to violence, vengeance, or hatred. He died loving..." (Ibid.) Above all in giving testimony to the true perspective of the Church's mission—one of love, and faith—the death of Grande, along with his campesino companions, was a gift to the Church of El Salvador. Romero considered the murder a crossroads in the history of El Salvador: a reminder to all that love can overcome violence, a powerful reminder for Salvadorans who were acutely suffering in the grips of that violence. (Ibid.)

With the intensification of the suffering in Rutilio's beloved parish of Our Lord of Mercies in Aguilares, the tragic infamy of Rutilio Grande's assassination continued to burden the Archbishop with grief and concern. Following the murder of Grande, who was the pastor in Aguilares, the Salvadoran military occupied the church and used it as barracks. For over two months following Rutilio's murder, and despite Romero's insistent demands that the church be vacated and returned to the archdiocese, the military continued its occupation of the sacred building.

Finally, on 19 June 1977 Archbishop Romero was allowed to re-enter the church's premises to reclaim it. As he addressed the parishioners, Romero declared his solidarity with the suffering and persecuted faithful people of Aguilares. Father Carranza recalls the archbishop proclaiming that "the voice of the prophet will remain vibrant."[5] While he did not name Grande specifically, the faithful parishioners understood Romero's reference to the prophet as their beloved Jesuit pastor Rutilio Grande. Romero confirmed that Aguilares itself has become:

> in the Archdiocese...a very special place, for it is here that Father Grande and his two beloved campesinos fell victim to the assassins' bullets. The direct persecution of the priest and the catechists is without any doubt a sign of the Lord's favor. (Ibid.)

Following the murder of Grande and companions, the courageous parishioners of Our Lord of Mercies in Aguilares continued to express their commitment to the Gospel, in spite of the on-going persecution that overtook their town. As Romero expressed it: "Here priests and lay people have literally handed their lives over to the Lord without thinking about martyrdom and suffering." (Ibid.) Romero affirmed that the testimony of Grande's life initiated a very bold movement that extended beyond the confines of Aguilares. It encouraged others to make a serious commitment to the crucified Christ just as Father Grande had done. Father Rutilio's example of life was giving birth to "heroes"—priests and catechists who boldly proclaimed the Gospel.

Once again Romero underscored the "originality" in the manner in which Christian liberation is lived, as the way Father Grande lived it: inspired and based on faith. Those engaged in a Christian understanding of liberation:

> resist the temptation of violence, hatred and resentment...love with the heart of Jesus...defend [one's] rights with love. Love is the power of the Church...never promoting hatred or class strug-

gle, for these are the powers of other false liberations that ultimately never lead to liberation. (Ibid.)

Romero's words captured the essence of Grande's Christian commitment and how the martyred pastor understood his priestly role in the Church. Grande had preached a message of human dignity and equality, particularly for the poor. According to Romero, because of Grande's efforts in Aguilares...

> people have discovered their rights and, in the light of Christ, defend these rights and must continue this struggle and also continue to be faithful to this illumination of faith and the teaching of the Church. (Ibid.)

Another legacy of the martyred priest was the courageous perseverance of his Jesuit brothers who continued in their labors to enlighten the campesinos. From their efforts, the vitality of Grande's ministry was resurrected anew. His life and death instilled the light of the Gospel in many hearts. Romero addressed his prayer to the new pastors of the future so that they might "know how to guide people along the true paths of Christian liberation and do so in a way that the Church desires." (Ibid.) The Medellín documents that Grande embraced provided the light that would lead the Latin American people to salvation; in this sense, Aguilares itself was a torch raised on high for all to see. (Ibid.)

In the years that followed, Romero remembered the martyred Grande on each anniversary of his death. In the archbishop's Sunday sermon (26 February 1978) as the first anniversary approached, the archbishop announced that the celebration would be held both in Grande's hometown of El Paisnal and in the cathedral of San Salvador. Romero noted:

> We have an obligation to remember the courage and commitment of Father Grande so that his voice which some people wanted to silence through violence might continue to cry out like Jesus: do not fear those who can kill only the body but leave the eternal Gospel and the Word alive in our midst.[6]

After a pause, the archbishop also spoke about the Mass remembrance for those who had died violently in the Plaza Libertad at the hands of the military when they had protested the fraudulent presidential election.[7] Again Romero alluded to Grande:

> The Lord desires that these prayers for Father Grande and his companions, as well as the suffrages for our other sisters and brothers who have died—the Lord wants these prayers to be understood as the true messages of the Church.[8]

As Romero had done in previous sermons, he stressed the unique feature of the Church's mission:

> Let it be very clear: the Church's objective is religious and from this religious perspective, this union with God, this prayer of hers, she derives her extension into the social, political and economic arenas...No one has the right to confuse the religious ends of the Church when they coincide with the temporal ends of their group.[9]

The archbishop had once again highlighted the unique character of Christian liberation that Rutilio exemplified.

A few days after Romero delivered this Sunday sermon in the Cathedral of San Salvador, he travelled to El Paisnal to celebrate the Mass for the first anniversary of Grande's death (5 March 1978). Romero proclaimed:

> Once again Christ is passing by El Paisnal. Each time that the Eucharist is celebrated, the Lord, as seen in today's gospel, passes by. This morning we are aware of the Lord's special passing and we want to interpret this event in the depths of our conscience, in our love and in our prayers for Father Grande and the two campesinos who died with him one year ago.[10]

On this special occasion, as was his custom, Romero based his sermon on Scripture with the clear intention to elucidate "why the Church views Father Grande as a great individual." (Ibid.) Romero spoke of Rutilio as a man, as a Christian and as a priest. He emphasized that it was critical to ensure that Rutilio's stature not be mutilated or twisted because he proclaimed an authentic liberation. (Ibid.) **The archbishop's exhortation promoted** the hope that those assembled for the anniversary celebration would continue to carry out the mission that Father Grande had carried out until his death. Romero is conscious of the legacy that Grande has left behind for others to continue.

As Romero spoke of Rutilio, he drew from the Scriptural account of the anointing of David as the future king of Israel. David, being the youngest son of Jesse and tending sheep in the fields, was the least likely to be selected by the Lord. In moving words, Romero reflected on the impoverishment of Rutilio's hometown and how despite outward appearances, this young campesino boy, like the biblical David, had been anointed by God. Romero pointed to Rutilio's greatest endowment:

> [T]his man carried from here the gift of love for his people. This man saw the landscape that we are seeing at this moment and like the children of today who live in Paisnal, felt the dust arise from the streets and experienced the sadness of poverty and the difficulties of living in a distant village. Yet this man also experienced the moral wealth of the people, the wealth of a home where he learned how to pray, where he learned how to see God and love the neighbor. (Ibid.)

Movingly, the archbishop stressed how Rutilio's humble beginning was, paradoxically, the source of his greatness and significantly instrumental in his human development. Although along his life's journey Father Grande had been blessed with many educational and cultural opportunities that contributed to his human flourishing, he never lost sight of the richness embedded in his childhood roots. Furthermore, in due time Father Grande had chosen to return to his home parish and there to live out his calling to its final moment. Romero, himself from a humble Salvadoran background, understood the significance of the role that one's "*tierra natal*" played in Rutilio Grande's development:

> [H]e became the man that we now claim as our own, the man whose teaching we want to embrace...Indeed, he was so human that it could appear that there was no other dimension to his life but this humanness. (Ibid.)

Having addressed Rutilio's humanity, Romero moved to recount the dimensions of Grande's spiritual life and Christian commitment.

At the age of thirteen, young Rutilio had felt a call by God to the priesthood. He answered the call when he first met Archbishop Luis Chávez y González. Despite the many challenges that Rutilio would inevitably encounter stemming from his impoverished background and his fragile health, Grande resolutely trusted in God to bring his call to fruition, or as Romero described it in his sermon: "...Rutilio was able to prostrate himself every day before the Lord and say: Yes, Lord, I believe in you; I will follow you." (Ibid.) Romero interpreted Rutilio's response to the call as that of a Christian who deeply believed in a liberation embedded in the gospel.

Contrary to the belief of others in Salvadoran society, Rutilio understood that gospel liberation promised the true progress for his people and nation.[11] By accepting this daunting challenge of faith, Grande began his journey toward martyrdom. Nevertheless, Father Rutilio assumed the challenge with courage in an on-going effort to "unmask so many evils"; for his stance, he was killed. His murderers believed that in taking Grande's life they had "put an end to Rutilio's Christian preaching." In fact, they laughed that, in the Catholic country of El Salvador, they had achieved the unique act of putting a priest to death. But, as Romero shared with those gathered at the first anniversary Mass for Father Rutilio and his companions, the archbishop discounted the "success" of the murders:

> What they did not expect was that his death would cause a storm, a spring time, and a new beginning that was initiated by the Christian people of El Salvador one year ago. (Ibid.)

Grande's death and the persecution of those in Aguilares and others that followed ignited in Christians a courage to face even death, if necessary. The Superior General of Jesuits promoted a comprehension similar to the archbishop's by pointing out that Grande's death was "the seed that produces more Christians and more vocations."[12] Others, like Father Octavio Cruz, former student and team member of Grande, shared this same sentiment,

> [T]hey were very difficult times, but very beautiful times. Because we, and I can testify that my colleagues and I, at no time were moved by any material interest, or any political ideology, but it was the pure Word of God and the documents of the Church. And we envisioned a Church committed to making what it said in its documents and what the Word of God was demanding for that difficult moment lived by the population. So, many of the Exodus situations at that time were spiritual situations that helped us to understand this situation and to discover the call God made.[13]

Once again, Romero had underscored the unique character of the Church's doctrine of liberation which was not to be confused with other liberations of the world. In the spirit of Gospel-based liberation Grande embraced the Christian commitment that led to his death as a martyr. At the anniversary Mass, Romero urged his listeners:

> Let us proclaim this doctrine from the perspective of knowing that one does not die when one is martyred, rather one rises above death and continues to become incarnated in the lives of those who follow.[14]

To conclude, the archbishop focused on Rutilio Grande as a priest and Jesuit. In living out his priestly vocation, Rutilio had early on chosen to enter the Society of Jesus. He had lived his religious commitment in the spirit of Saint Ignatius responding to three major questions: "What have I done for Christ? What do I do for Christ? What should I do for Christ?" (Ibid.) The archbishop reiterated that the humble people Father Grande had served taught the answers to the questions:

> [H]e learned how to be a Christian because you, the people of El Salvador, showed him the true image of Christ that Saint Ignatius spoke about. This image of Christ is not only discovered during a spiritual retreat, but is also found here, living among the people where Christ is enfleshed and suffers, where Christ is persecuted, where Christ is found in men who sleep in the fields because

they are unable to sleep in their houses, where Christ is seen in the sick and those who suffer the consequences of so many painful conditions. (Ibid.)

Rutilio had seen the crucified Christ incarnated in the faces of the poor, and had sought to alleviate their misery. For this he had been killed, and Romero sees that by his death Grande had been anointed with the oil of martyrdom.

Those left behind inherit Rutilio Grande's gifts as a precious trust to continue his commitment. Romero is clear, however, that the commitment is not to the person of Father Rutilio, but to Jesus who is at the heart of that Christian commitment. In sharing the holy baptism of the faithful, Romero invited those assembled to embrace the example of the martyr of El Paisnal. In words meant to instruct and inspire the people of Aguilares and El Paisnal, Romero shared a personal sentiment, revealing, perhaps, the deep emotion that still moved him:

> Now here, with his brother priests around the altar, we say that we miss him. We feel as though he should be walking with us and that someone was killed who should not have suffered such a fate. We feel as though he should be walking with us and doing good. He was so strong, so young! He could have done so much. (Ibid.)

This legacy is soaked in a martyr's blood, and it is "the memory of him [that] will bring hope to our people if we know how to understand the Christian and priestly dimensions of his life." (Ibid.) Again, Romero profiled Rutilio as a martyr who was not only anointed with the oil of chrism at his ordination, but then, with his death, was anointed with the oil of martyrdom: his own blood." (Ibid.) The archbishop affirmed that by remembering Rutilio Grande, his presence will live on in the people as a source of hope and guidance.

From the tone of Romero's sermon, there is little doubt that the death of Father Rutilio had touched Romero at the core of his heart. For the subsequent three years until his own martyred death, Archbishop Romero always remembered his friend Rutilio on the anniversary of his death. On 11 March 1979 as the second anniversary drew near, Romero called attention to those attending the Sunday Mass in the Cathedral that at that same moment in Aguilares, the faithful were organizing a memorial procession to El Paisnal. The archbishop reminded his congregation that Father Grande had called similar gatherings "Manifestations of Faith"—a way of demonstrating how Christians were called to confront the injustices of society.

Rutilio's last such manifestation had been at Apopa when he and others gathered to protest the kidnapping, torture, and exile of Father Bernal. Perhaps, that image stirred in Romero's mind as he spoke of the gathering for Grande as:

> one of silence and prayer—a procession that defines us as a people of prayer and reflection as we honor the memory of Father Rutilio Grande who was assassinated two years ago.[15]

Speaking as Archbishop from the pulpit in the Cathedral of San Salvador, Romero enjoined all the faithful to unite themselves in a spirit of prayer and gratitude to that procession in El Paisnal for Father Rutilio and for all those who boldly proclaim the gospel as he had done. The witness of his life had left in Aguilares, "a Church marked with the seal of authenticity."(Ibid.) Romero reminded all Christians, in Aguilares and elsewhere, that the anniversary procession was one of faith, hope and love; that persecution not only gave meaning to the Christian life, but was a mark of the true Church of Jesus Christ. (Ibid.) Every Christian, he explained, was called to accompany the Church in good and also in difficult times. Theirs is a Church and a nation that is being invited to transform the violent and evil realities that they were living. While in this homily Romero does not speak extensively of Grande, it seems that, given his references to the times and circumstances in which the Church was living, the memory of Rutilio Grande inspired his words.

In this lengthy Sunday address, Romero mentioned Grande with two additional allusions. He recalled the figure of the prophet Elijah who also lived during a time of "crimes, distortions of the truth, political manipulations, bribes that supported injustice, abuse of wealth and money" (Ibid.): a situation similar to those that the priests in El Paisnal were experiencing. Facing his land's corrosive realities, Elijah simply wanted to die. Even in its brevity, Romero parallels Rutilio Grande as a persistent man who believed above all in God's faithfulness. Aligning Grande with similar scriptural figures, Romero encouraged everyone to believe in the impossible.

At another moment in the sermon, Romero highlighted the difference between civil destabilization and the demands of Christian conscience:

> The Church must awaken the conscience to dignity, but this is called subversion. With the light of the Gospel, our Christian communities are awakening to the truth that every person, even the most humble worker, is an image of God—this is not communism or subversion, rather it is the Word of God which illuminates the human person and so people must promote this idea. (Ibid.)

The archbishop's words echoed the same beliefs that Grande held and which he promoted in his early ministry and later in the rural ministry in Aguilares and surrounding villages. Before ending this homily, Romero made a final mention of the community procession to El Paisnal in honor of their martyred pastor and asked his listeners to join them spiritually.

Romero reiterated that Church was "not built to remain hidden in some closet, to be a Church that is confined to the sacristy. Indeed the Church is established to be firm and to enlighten and serve and shine forth upon the world." (Ibid.) The archbishop's words coincided precisely with Grande's perspective, one which he had explicated in an article for *El Mundo*,[16] one of the local newspapers. In the Cathedral earlier that anniversary morning, funeral services had been held for another young man. Mentioning the young age of the deceased, Romero lamented that Rutilio, too, had died too young, only forty-nine when he was assassinated. Although in this final Sunday homily Romero did not speak directly or at length about Father Rutilio, the Archbishop's words resonated palpably with the martyred priest's memory, thoughts and beliefs.

On three different occasions during March of 1980, as the third anniversary of the death of Rutilio Grande drew near, Romero explicitly remembered Grande. On the first Sunday of that month, the archbishop informed his Sunday listeners that the community of Aguilares was suffering great difficulties as they prepared for Grande's anniversary. Since the assassination of their pastor, the town had increasingly become a target of repression. The safety of those intending to participate in the memorial Mass was a serious concern. In spite of the fact that three years had passed since Grande's murder, the oppression of the town had intensified rather than abated.

In a few brief statements, the archbishop affirmed that Grande was not only the first martyr of El Salvador, but that he belonged to the country.[17] The mission of the Church of El Salvador was to "speak about social, political and economic realities because it [had] to enlighten these realities with the light of the gospel."(Ibid.) As Romero had reminded the faithful of San Salvador in previous Sunday homilies:

> [P]ersecution is a characteristic mark of the authentic Church. A Church that does not suffer persecution is not the true church of Jesus Christ. This does not mean that martyrdom and suffering and fear and persecution are normal but rather all of these realities ought to give meaning to the Christian spirit. (Ibid.)

The people of Aguilares, evangelized by Father Grande, continued to live out their Christian commitment despite the cost. As was his custom, during the Mass Romero recounted the violent events of the previous week and enumerated the incidents of assault on the citizenry of San Salvador. Among the atrocities the archbishop included the discovery of the bodies of slain students and campesinos from El Paisnal, Grande's hometown. A true sign of the authenticity of Grande's "martyrdom" was the fact that the faithful of Aguilares whom he had evangelized were suffering persecution. As the Church of El Salvador opted for the preferential love for the poor, it increasingly became a target of a repressive violence.

The following Sunday, Archbishop Romero took time during his homily to announce that later that morning he would be in Aguilares concelebrating at the anniversary celebration of Grande's death. Although by then the persecution was widespread throughout El Salvador, the town of Aguilares continued to be a special object of cruelty. Romero read from a desperate letter that he received:

> I beg you to ask the individuals who govern our country to please cease the persecution that we have endured. I and my family have been threatened on many occasions and the only reason for this is that we were friends of Father Rutilio Grande. The authorities threaten us and tell us that we are guerrillas; and again, this has occurred because we have known Father Rutilio.[18]

Romero cited information he received that there had been forty new victims in Aguilares. (Ibid.) While honoring his friend Rutilio in the Mass was important, for the archbishop it was imperative to denounce the assaults that had occurred that week. He addressed the oligarchy, government officials, revolutionary coordinators of the masses, and the guerrilla groups. As a minister of the Church Archbishop Romero felt called to work for the reconciliation of opposing groups in the country.

On 23 March 1980, the final Sunday before his own murder, Romero delivered a homily entitled: "The Church in the Service of Personal, Community and Transcendent Liberation." He reported that at the previous week's anniversary Mass for Grande in Aguilares, fear had kept many people away.[19] This was the last time that Archbishop Romero would be able to speak of Father Rutilio Grande. It is also interesting to note, that Romero referred to the event not as the anniversary of Father Grande's death, but the anniversary of Grande's assassination.

In spotlighting the circumstances of his fellow priest's murder, the archbishop drew attention both to the deteriorating Catholicism of a country that considered the murder of a priest an acceptable sport, as well as to the general disregard for life that had become the norm. In concluding this homily, he appealed directly to the army's enlisted men, pleading for them to stop the killing of their own brothers and sisters, and to stop the repression. (Ibid.) The very following day, Romero himself was gunned down as he celebrated Mass in the chapel of La Divina Providencia. In death, he joined the friend that he had cherished in life. Archbishop Romero's death would be remembered each anniversary of his assassination, just as he had done for Rutilio Grande.

Perspective

After the murder of Jesuit Rutilio Grande, Archbishop Óscar Arnulfo Romero dedicated time in his homilies to remember his friend. As already mentioned, he did so on eight separate occasions between 1977 and 1980. Each homily contains multiple insights into what Romero thought of Grande. Their relationship has been a subject of interest for writers and biographers.[20] Without a doubt, Romero was a gifted preacher. His homilies are an inexhaustible treasure that merit ongoing analysis and examination. What is offered here is an initial exploration and consideration of what can be gleaned from Romero's homilies on Rutilio Grande.

Romero's Personal Relationship

Popular belief about these two priests and martyrs of El Salvador is that they enjoyed a profound friendship. Although there is definite evidence that they were friends, the extent of that relationship has not been fully established. What can be seen in Romero's homilies is the archbishop's affection, respect, and admiration for the younger man. Romero's homily delivered at Father Rutilio's funeral opened with the sentiments of a grieving brother who chose not to focus on his personal loss, but rather on the meaning of Grande's death for the Church and the country of El Salvador. Nevertheless, each year as the anniversary of Grande's death approached, during Eucharistic celebrations in the Cathedral presided over by the archbishop, Romero remembered Rutilio publicly. In particular, the homily marking the first anniversary of Rutilio's death, reveals Romero's intimate knowledge of Grande's life from his childhood to his death. And, on that first anniversary, Romero spoke of the void left behind in the hearts of Rutilio's brother priests as well as his own. As Romero expressed it: "...a man of such great hope has been taken from us."[21] In that familiar sense of mourning experienced by all of us who have suffered the loss of a loved one, Romero still

found it unimaginable that Rutilio has died.

Role of the Church

Throughout Romero's homilies in which he mentions Rutilio and the meaning of his death, Romero examined the role of the Church. At Father Rutilio's funeral Mass, Romero, citing Paul VI's document of *Evangelization in the Modern World*, affirmed that in life his friend was exercising the role of the Church in the struggle for liberation from misery. As the Church advanced its obligation to cry out on behalf of those who suffered poverty and were deprived of human dignity, Grande had committed himself to that struggle, especially on behalf of the poor. In all of his pastoral endeavors, the young Jesuit had devoted himself to helping others realize their human dignity.

Rutilio was well educated in the social teachings of the Church and drew the inspiration for his own pastoral work from them. The dynamic of his commitment was driven by basic Church teaching: faith in Jesus Christ requires responding to the needs of the world without being aligned with the power of political parties. He loved the Church and shared the belief that its mission to the poor and marginalized possessed a unique character. Grande's integrated fidelity to the social teachings of the Church was repeatedly acknowledged in the homilies that Romero delivered about his brother priest and friend. Romero profoundly understood Father Grande's commitment. In fact, among those who knew Rutilio, his Christian commitment to justice for the poor was an outstanding aspect of his life.

Characterization of Grande

In a remarkable moment during Grande's funeral Mass and on other occasions as well, Romero referred to Grande as a "martyr." In fact, Romero acknowledged his special place in the universal Church as the "first martyr" of El Salvador. The archbishop considered the circumstances of Grande's life and death appropriate to bestow this sacred accolade: one who died for the faith in the defense of the poor. Father Rutilio, Romero affirmed, was not only anointed with the oil of martyrdom, but lived as a prophet who announced the Good News and denounced the evil that impoverished the humanity of the dispossessed of his country and the world. In his own humanity, Rutilio Grande's physical and emotional health was fragile; but in carrying out his priestly ministry, he was fearless, courageous. These were characteristics of Grande that Romero reflected upon in several of his homilies. He speaks of Rutilio's courage, commitment, and giftedness in teaching the Gospel to those entrusted to his care. Romero reminds his listeners that Rutilio Grande's life served as an example, inspiration and gift to his fellow Jesuits, to the Church and to the faithful. Furthermore, he asserts that Grande fully deserved the gratitude of all those he served both within the institutional Church and throughout the countryside of El Salvador.

Humanity

Romero understood the forces that shaped Rutilio Grande into the man that he became. In particular, he credited Grande's humble beginnings in El Paisnal as the major influence in shaping the pastor as a man of his people. Romero understood Rutilio as a person who in striving to become fully human, was graced with a capacity to see the face of the Crucified Christ in the poor. Grande's humanity also enabled him to understand the humanity of others. He drew from the deep well of his childhood history of poverty and deprivation to find in that experience, a source of grace for himself and others. At the same time, Grande had tasted the simple joys offered by his hometown of El Paisnal, and understood that one's humanity was not defined by wealth.

Incarnation

As a man who was shaped by his humble beginnings, Grande had a remarkable ability to connect the experience of his youth to that of the rural people he served. Seminarians who had been his students testified that he had the gift to make the Word of God come alive in the historical context of one's time and place. He presented the Gospel in the reality of El Salvador, and in death, he continued to live in the lives of those he had served. His murderers rejoiced that they had silenced Father Rutilio. On the contrary, however, he became an even greater force for those who knew him or heard about the witness of his death. His martyrdom inspired the Church to embrace a new and unique manner of preaching the Gospel in its preferential option for the poor. As Romero proclaimed, Rutilio's death: "... cause[d] a storm, a springtime, and a new beginning that was initiated by the Christian people of El Salvador."[22]

Memory and Legacy

The power of memory is evident throughout Romero's homilies. The simple act of speaking about Grande was a courageous reminder of who this Jesuit pastor had been and what he stood for in the history of the Church and Republic of El Salvador. As the celebration of the Eucharist makes Jesus present, uttering the name of Rutilio Grande, restored him from the dead and made him present. The witness of his life and death gave courage and inspiration to countless women and men who toil to change unjust systems. Father Rutilio Grande's legacy was multifaceted. As Romero said "...he was so human that it could appear that there was no other dimension to his life but this humanness."

And in profound ways, Rutilio's humanity is central to his legacy. Because early on Grande embraced his human limitations with all its challenges, he opened himself to the embrace of God and of the people he served. His humanity was the well from which he drew his relationship to God and suffering humanity. His faith in God's compassionate love imbued him with the strength that he needed to carry out his Christian commitment. His trust in God's unfailing love gave him the courage to preach the Gospel despite the cost. Grande also believed in the capacity of each human being to become more human if given the right circumstances. The ministerial method that he developed honored the human potential of those entrusted to his pastoral care. He reinforced a new understanding of Church as inspired by the Second Vatican Council and Medellín. He did not live to see that vision wholly realized, but his memory and witness inspire others to strive to do so.

As Romero reasserted: "We are a pilgrim Church, exposed to misunderstanding and persecution, but we are a Church that walks calmly because we carry within us this power of love."[23]

NOTES

1. See: "Vatican: Oscar Romero is 'a martyr' of the church of the Second Vatican Council, National Catholic Reporter, 4 February 2015.
2. Romero, "Dedicated Love," 14 March 1977 homily. RTW, accessed 2017.
3. Paraphrasing *Evangelii nuntiandi* §30.
4. "Dedicated Love." The following two quotations in the next several paragraphs are also from this homily.
5. Romero, "A Torch Raised on High," 19 June 1977 homily. RTW, accessed 2017. The next five quotations in the next several paragraphs are also from this homily.
6. Romero, "Redemption, From God Via Christ to All," 26 February 1978 homily. RTW, accessed 2017.
7. See: Ana Maria Pineda, *Romero & Grande: Companions on the Journey*, 135.
8. "Redemption, From God Via Christ to All."
9. Ibid.
10. Romero, "Rutilio Grande: Man, Christian, Priest" 5 March 1978 homily. RTW, accessed 2017. The quotations in the next several paragraphs are also from this homily.
11. See again: "Rutilio Grande: Man, Christian, Priest." The three quotations following in this paragraph are taken from this same homily.
12. Ibid. Quoted in Romero's sermon, "Rutilio Grande: Man, Christian, Priest."
13. Interview with Father Octavio Cruz, 2015.
14. Rutilio Grande: Man, Christian, Priest." The four quotations in the next several paragraphs are also taken from this homily.
15. Romero, "Lent, the Transfiguration of God's People," 11 March 1979 homily. RTW, accessed 2017. The quotations in the next several paragraphs are also from this homily.
16. *El Mundo*, "Lo Social también es de Competencia de la Iglesia," 8 May 1970
17. Romero, "Conversion, Requisite for True Liberation," 9 March 1980 homily. RTW, accessed 2017. The following two quotations are also from this homily.
18. Romero, "Reconciliation in Christ, True Liberation," 16 March 1980 homily. RTW, accessed 2017.
19. Romero, "The Church in the Service of Personal, Community and Transcendent Liberation, 23 March 1980 homily. RTW, accessed 2017.
20. Rodolfo Cardenal, S.J. and a few others have written on the topic of the homilies that Archbishop Romero delivered on Rutilio Grande, SJ and their significance. What I have written reflects my own thinking on the content of Romero's homilies and what his words might reveal on what he thought about Grande. Without a doubt, the archbishop's homilies are rich and my work does not exhaust the richness of his words and thought.
21. "Rutilio Grande: Man, Christian, Priest."
22. Ibid. The quotation at the end of the next paragraph is also from this homily.
23. Romero, "Dedicated Love."

CHAPTER 5

MEMORY AND LEGACY

Having explored Rutilio Grande's homilies, writings, and correspondence and seeing an image of the man revealed in the sermons of Archbishop Óscar Romero, we ponder the question: Who was this man? Although decades have passed since his death, his memory and presence have become a rich legacy for the people of El Salvador and many others beyond the borders of this small country. What exactly is the legacy of the Jesuit Rutilio Grande?

There are many ways to consider the question. One approach is to gather the voices of those who knew Rutilio Grande and whose memories are still vivid and vibrant. Shared stories and remembrances, his words sung in hymns and folk ballads or painted within colorful murals on neighborhood walls throughout El Salvador all speak of Rutilio Grande, a man of the people. This final chapter aims to assemble precious memories that reveal and delineate the legacy he left for people everywhere to pursue justice in the spirit of the Gospel to make this a better world.

Rutilio Grande, the Man

As is true of every human being, Rutilio's life reflects a multifaceted person. Interestingly enough, it is the smiling image of Grande that surfaces in the memory of some. "If you spoke with Father Rutilio Grande, you wouldn't know whether he had celebrated Mass, if he had prayed, or where he was coming from. He always arrived with that smile..."[1] His smile seems to be one of his most noticeable physical characteristics. Although attached to neatly attired clerical garb, which for some came across as markedly conservative, it was his smile that came across as one of the outstanding qualities that he possessed.[2] He was a man that maintained good relationships with those he ministered and lived. As one of his former seminarians commented, "We could never accuse him of treating others poorly. No. We can remember him as a smiling priest that gave us permission, and listened to us with openness to dialogue."[3]

For those that he embraced in his ministry in Aguilares, one of the salient qualities he possessed was his humanness:

> Even more than being a priest, he was a priest who was human. Like family, a father of a family, [he was] sincere when he spoke, and in [his] treating [of] us. He was totally open with all of us... And he ate alongside us. The missionaries arrived to the hamlets to eat beans. It was what we had, and that was what they had to eat...[4]

In fact, Rutilio's presence among the campesinos offered them a new example of the priesthood. Manuel Quijano, a parishioner from Aguilares, commented, "They did not eat separately, but with us. When had we ever seen a priest with us in this way, that was very pleasing for all the people."[5] Rutilio mingled freely with those he met throughout his many years of ministry. One of his former seminarians describes him,

> He wasn't a recluse. Although, I think that he was apparently timid. And, I mean timid in the sense that he wasn't naturally spontaneous. But, his timidity had a gentleness to it. He wasn't a man of great splendor. But his smile won over many.[6]

For the seminarians who were used to the faculty being predominantly priests from Spain, Rutilio being one of their own stood out. Miguel Ventura describes him:

> He was the closest figure we felt in the seminary. He was always present. I remember him walking around the halls at many hours of the day, of the night. At that moment, I'll tell you, he manifested a temperament, I believe, shy. Shy. It was natural. Many of us come from peasant environments, and that greatly influenced our personalities.

However, it was a shyness that did not limit him. But, the man, then, with his own personality was dealing with problems, but perhaps he didn't approach them in an impulsive manner.[7]

Grande enjoyed those he met during his many years of ministry. He was approachable. "He was a man who would dialogue, a man open to it. And, when he had to demand discipline, he also did so."[8] His responsibilities as prefect of discipline in the seminary required that he help the seminarians under his care to see their errors. But, he did not scold. Instead, he would say his piece and ask the seminarian in question to give his point of view.[9] Grande had a great concern for the individual needs of people. He liked the seminarians to dress nicely. For example, he drew from his childhood days and often said "Although it is patched, it is clean."[10] This popular saying spoke to the person's dignity despite the scarcity of fancy clothing. In Rutilio's experience, it wasn't the outer clothing that made the person worthwhile. At the same time, there was a dignity in his demeanor. As some described him, Father Grande was tall of medium build who carried himself with dignity.[11] While he was born into poverty, that in no way had to determine the worth of a person, as was reflected in his gait and demeanor. Antonio Ocaña, who knew Grande from his early Jesuit formation, describes him as:

> He was a man more drawn to shyness than being very communicative. Very quiet. Very polite. Very kind ... elegant ... very affectionate with people, with the campesinos, and with us seminarians as well.[12]

In his work ethic, Grande was a man who "...when he started something, he liked to proceed step-by-step. He did not like disorder. He did not like to skip steps. It was part of his character and his way of being. He would tell the students, "We start with this; we continue with the other until it is finalized."[13] From this, those who worked with him learned that it was not necessarily a matter of finishing the task, but it was important to begin the work to see where it would take one. Grande was a seeker.[14] He encouraged discussion and defended the seminarians in their new approaches to ministry and their evolving understanding of themselves as future priests. "He was, as one could say, that nice mediator, sympathetic that defended those new attitudes of ours that for many seemed scandalous."[15] When hearing complaints about the young seminarians, he would say, "Look, Monseñor, that's the most normal thing. We live in another time."[16] He was always in search of a better understanding.

Whether he was teaching in the classroom or with the campesinos of his parish, his teaching approach was orderly, imaginative, and empowering. Grande taught them about a God who was relevant and alive in the world. Many had received basic catechetical instruction but listening to Rutilio helped them discover a personal God who accompanied his people in the daily circumstances of life.

From another's perspective: "He was a man of integrity."[17] As one of the Delegates of the Word recalled, on one occasion, Father Grande refused a gift of flowers brought to the parish church by three local women of wealth, whom he knew paid their workers unjustly. As he told them,

> You are lost. Because you want to look good with God, but you are going wrong with your brothers. From this moment, I forbid you to come and leave flowers here. Because that money with which you buy those flowers, it's not what you have. It's what you steal from the workers, and God doesn't want that.[18]

For the better part of his priestly life, Grande engaged in serious matters affecting the life of the campesinos. He did not sing or play musical instruments, yet he found joy in the mischievousness of the seminarians and enjoyed their youthful jokes.[19] He was always fond of the typical popular food enjoyed by Salvadorans. He ensured that whenever there was a festivity in the seminary that typical fare was prepared for them.[20]

His fragile health was always a concern and an object of speculation. As noted in his biography, early on in his Jesuit life, Grande suffered what was described by his biographer, Rodolfo Cardenal, as a "catatonic episode."[21] In a few of his personal letters, Rutilio references this health condition. But, it was a condition that he tried to keep to himself. Even his family was unaware of it, and from some accounts, few perceived it. When asked about it, Octavio Cruz, a former student of Grande in the seminary and later a team member in Aguilares, recalled,

> I could not perceive something like that, but rather what I saw was more like the inner struggle of anyone trying to be faithful. I felt that it was like the testimony of a person who is wanting to be faithful to his charisma and what God is asking. It might be that those who knew him well noted that he had a problem of this kind that required treatment or something else.[22]

But, Cruz noted that while Father Rutilio was a man of a balanced disposition, he insisted on taking a brief daily nap.[23] Otherwise, according to Rutilio, "If I don't have a nap, I have a bad afternoon."[24]

However, other Jesuit friends and collaborators were keenly aware of Grande's fragile disposition that manifested in bouts of depression and self-doubt. Salvador Carranza, S.J., a lifetime friend and team member, often listened to his Jesuit friend fret (agonize) about a pending ministerial responsibility or other situations as Carranza notes:

> [Rutilio] always had various problems. But not when it was time for him to speak in public, no. Then he was transformed, and he placed himself in the place of those to whom he was talking… and no doubt came out. This was an example of doubting. [He would ask others] This or this? It was very, very, very typical of him. To walk around filled with doubts, he consulted a lot. From Aguilares, he would often travel to talk to the teachers of the UCA about what the peasants were doing. He would ask whether to take this direction or insist on this.[25]

Rutilio learned to live with this condition, as noted in the biographical information written by the Centroamerican Province of the Society of Jesus and kept in their archives in San Salvador:

> At the beginning of his religious life, he manifested a clear nervous weakness. He had psy-

> chological depressions and it was feared for his mental health. He was aware of that limitation, suffered for it, but he did not let it control him; He accepted it. He worked to dominate it, and he overcame it.
>
> Perhaps because of this illness, his natural qualities did not shine so much. Maybe this disease was the reason why Rutilio was able to control outbursts and impulses, and put himself more securely, and with utter simplicity, in the hands of God."[26]

In the words of Octavio Cruz: "... with more reason God's work manifested itself in a better way. Because despite the limitations, he was able to fulfill the mission, and he was able to respond to what the Lord asked of him."[27] At no other time was it more apparent that Rutilio Grande was filled with God's spirit than when he preached:

> ... there in the parish of Aguilares, I was able, therefore, to experience this dimension... of how Rutilio was transformed. One was the Rutilio when we were talking in meetings, to the Rutilio that when he was in the homily was a man full of God, with a strength, with a capacity to communicate and to be understood by the people, [speaking] with a simple language, a popular language, but also with a great bravery to denounce sin and injustices.[28]

This is the description of Rutilio Grande preserved in the memories of men and women who knew him. Despite the passage of time, the image of Rutilio Grande emerges with ease. And, what about his other contributions? Perhaps, those can be found in exploring several dimensions of his work: 1) Formation of Seminarians, Laity; 2) Religiosity of the People; 3) Ministry Approach; 4) New Model of Church; and 5) Gift of Martyrdom.

Formation of Seminarians

Beginning in 1960, Rutilio had several occasions to be involved in seminary formation. After his ordination and completion of theology in Oña, Spain, the young priest was assigned for two years to the Seminary of San José de la Montaña in San Salvador as professor of Latin and American History, while also serving as the prefect of discipline in the minor seminary. In 1962, he left the seminary to continue his Jesuit formation, along with a year of study at Lumen Vitae in Brussels.

In 1965, he once again returned to the seminary in San Salvador to serve as prefect of discipline and professor of pastoral theology and field work (1965-1970). For the next five years, the creative ministerial imagination of Father Grande would transform the traditional formation of the seminary to something more attuned to the directives of the Second Vatican Council. As Father Octavio Cruz, of the diocese of San Salvador, commented:

> It is true that he [Rutilio] had been formed before the Vatican Council, but he had an open mind to the Second [Vatican] Council... That God of the Bible who gives the answer to the human condition, it was that God that we now encountered in the sacraments.[29]

Father Rutilio was a dedicated professor and demonstrated a talent for communicating the subject matter at hand. He also had a vision for priestly formation that was more attuned with contemporary realities and the spirit of the Second Vatican Council. The seminarians would experience a new formation ushered in by Grande. Miguel Ventura, a seminarian taught by Father Rutilio in those years, considered the new approach to be:

> ... in such a way that this training will take us all the seminarians to open the doors of the seminary. The seminary was quite closed with that conception of Trent, right? We must train the priests, therefore, in an environment, I will say, doctrinally, ecclesiastically very enclosed, extremely enclosed. But Rutilio Grande's thought was different. He believed that there can be no salvific and liberating evangelization, if the future priest does not come into contact with reality. Then, Rutilio Grande, I think, is the one that opens also doors ahead of its times so that we

could have in the process of our pastoral planning an analysis of the country's reality. An analysis of the ecclesial reality. An analysis, if you want, of the Latin American reality. But all this, for what? For this evangelization to have a framework, a transformative framework of reality.[30]

In light of this expressed desire to make the seminarians aware of the reality that people were living outside of the seminary walls, as part of their pastoral exposure Grande introduced a new formation opportunity to take the young men to the surrounding communities. It was an innovative plan to have the seminarians visit the communities during the weekends and/or vacation time. Before embarking on the visits, Father Rutilio would prepare the seminarians instructing them on the listening attitude that they should have when they visited the families. In particular, they should be attentive to what the people shared with them during the visits and what they observed. Upon their return to the seminary, the students would meet to identify and analyze the people's realities, and based on their discovery design the appropriate pastoral approach.[31]

The process itself gave the seminarians an opportunity to discover their personal leadership skills. Some of the students were placed in charge of overseeing the process along with their classmates. All were involved in gathering the data they collected during the visits and in the process of analyzing and drawing ministerial conclusions. Throughout it, the seminarians gained confidence in their ability to respond to the needs of the communities they would someday serve. Rutilio Sanchez reminisced,

> I was in charge of planning. Of course, along with him [Grande]. It was my turn to collect all the daily experiences, order them, systematize them. And, together with a team we had formed from the same companions, we drew conclusions. That was important to me. It was a very nice experience because it helped me to discover some of one's own organizational abilities.[32]

Another student recalled how he felt valued and appreciated by Father Rutilio. At the same time, he also knew that, when necessary, Grande would demand more especially when he felt his students could do more to reach their potential. Father Cruz recalled such an occasion when he was a young student. He was given a low grade by Rutilio and was told:

> This is good, but you have more capacity. That's why I gave you "7". Not because it was bad, but because he said you can do more. And I remember that I did not feel bad, but I felt challenged and appreciated. Because I knew he liked me. I mean, he had a lot of confidence and hope that I would be a good priest.[33]

Aside from the immersion experiences in the outlying communities Grande made the seminary a location for theological and ministerial learning. Along with the educational events that Grande hosted, great care was given to the liturgy imbued by the spirit of renovation brought about by the Second Vatican Council. Or as Carranza expresses:

> It was [in the seminary] that Rutilio distinguished himself... He along with new seminary professors held the belief that "You have to change this or you have to update it." That was Rutilio's belief. This also applied to the seminarians who had to be formed for today and according to the Council and the Episcopal Conference of Medellín.[34]

Rutilio Grande was contributing to the formation of a new kind of priest for a new time in the Church and in El Salvador. Or as his former student, Miguel Ventura shares:

> If there is a key man in the formation of this new clergy [it is Rutilio Grande]. One need only to look at the fruits of his labor, the results, all this generation of heroes, of priests martyrs, they were the ones who lived with him in formation.[35]

Grande excelled in seminary formation. The process of formation that he used in the seminary would serve Father Rutilio as he embraced the directives of the Second Vatican Council to engage in the evangelization of the people he would serve in the parish of Our Lord of Mercies in Aguilares.

A New Model of Church

Some of the pastoral and ministerial concerns that were reflected in Father Grande's work had previously been undertaken by other priests in the diocese of San Salvador.[36] But his work in the seminary was countercultural. Its novelty eventually led to his dismissal from the seminary by the bishops who found it problematic and going against what had been traditionally regarded as the proper way of forming priests.

However, Rutilio's pastoral insight and approach was responding to the Vatican Council II's directive to be attentive to the signs of the times and to align priestly formation with its spirit. Looking back, Miguel Ventura commented on the formative years of Grande's pastoral work with the seminarians:

> But the man was overseeing all of it. He was like driving this whole process. He was laying the foundations for a new vision, of a liberating faith. We cannot have a salvation in history, or build a history of salvation, if we do not come into contact with reality. And that's what shaped, to a large extent, our disposition, our character, our vision, right? How to build in El Salvador a Church of the People. Because it was also building that Church of the People, but also enabling people to become their own agents in the promotion of this Church, and bringing about these changes, in the light of the faith.[37]

Father Grande promoted this creation of a new Church not only through adopting a new approach to the formation of clergy, but also in the formation of lay men and women. It was in Aguilares that the young pastor would engage in a new pastoral approach. Eva Menjivar accompanied Grande's pastoral team. From her perspective, she observed,

> I think that Father Grande was a very enlightened man of God. One could say, filled with all the spirit of Jesus. That revolutionized all the journey of the communities. And, communities were created in all the hamlets...[38]

Grande often voiced his belief: "Now, we're not going to do

it anymore, we're not going to wait for missionaries from the outside, right? Rather, we must be our own missionaries."[39] In this spirit, Rutilio, along with three other Jesuit confreres, began to visit the hamlets in the outskirts of Aguilares, as well as the people in the town. After a fifteen-day visit, eventually teams consisting of priests and lay people were formed. The diverse responsibilities to carry out the life of the Christian communities were assigned to those possessing that skill and talent. As word spread of this mission effort, some people were encouraged to attend the Eucharist or bible study that were celebrated. Manuel Quijano, resident of Potrero Grande, was drawn by the lively celebration of the Mass. He eagerly waited to meet Father Rutilio who was expected to visit a nearby hamlet. Although Quijano could neither read nor write, the news of this new undertaking was infectious. He was determined to attend.

> I hadn't been to school. I couldn't recognize the alphabet. There was nothing else I knew; I could not read anything. But, I said, please God, if they come here to Potrero Grande, I said to myself, I must see how I get a Bible. And, I was "blessed" by God because when they got there, I was the very first one who received a book.[40]

Quijano was selected by the community as a Delegate of the Word. He also taught himself to read following the painstaking method of trying to identity each word until he understood the sentence. Father Grande taught the people how to study the Bible. Because he knew the reality of their lives, he knew how to help them learn. According to Eva Menjivar, Grande was "a simple man, very sensible, very humble... He would tell the people: "We are going to study a grand chapter. We are going to think that this grand chapter is a hacienda—and that the verses are hectares or small pieces of land that you are responsible to work."[41] To others, Rutilio would assign the reading of an entire book in the Bible to read, and when they commented on the length, Grande responded:

> Read it slowly, interpret as you go along. Don't just read for the sake of reading it. Chew on what you read. Think and talk about what you think.

> For only in this way will you come to know Christ, and Christ will come to know you. You are going to be servants of Christ. You are not going to be someone else's servant. You are not going to be mine. You belong to Christ. But you have to be prepared… And this is our mission.[42]

Grande's approach and leadership in the formation of the laity in the parish of Aguilares was so effective that, in 1974 alone, there were 362 Delegates of the Word. As the process of evangelization unfolded, the people began to seek just compensation for their hard work. The people approached Father Rutilio and expressed their will to him:

> Well, we want to organize ourselves as campesinos. Because if we do not organize ourselves, we have no right to ask for what we need. And the Gospel itself is demanding that we have to demand justice. What we are living is an injustice.[43]

This would eventually lead them to organize to fight for the rights of the rural workers. And, in the wake of his death, Rutilio Grande's words would be actualized in many of their lives:

> [Jesus told the apostles] Because of me, you are going to suffer, you are going to be persecuted, you are going to be jailed. You will be clubbed and expelled from your communities, and you will even be killed, but do not worry. For Jesus Christ himself said, "He who gives his life for his people and for the Gospel has eternal life."[44]

This new way of being Church had given birth to an innovative approach to ministry. It was a very enriching experience because it was an experience of planned and organized work, with a defined methodology. The missions were the method to evangelize the people and to also have them become active agents in the process of their own evangelization. The priest, along with the lay women and women of the diverse communities, shared in the distribution of tasks.[45] All was shared. Even after Father Grande's death, the people shared in the ultimate price of discipleship.

Religiosity of the People

Following the spirit of the Second Vatican Council and Medellín, in introducing a new model of Church, Father Grande also gave privileged attention to the role of the laity in the Church and in the world. In doing so, he also acknowledged the merit of their way of life and religious sensibilities. Popular practices that had either been dismissed as misguided forms of religiosity by the clergy and/or elite were reconsidered as authentic expressions of faith.

In Aguilares, Rutilio insisted that the work of the team be shaped by the people's faith. One of the traditional religious celebrations that he highlighted and transformed was that of the Festival of the Corn (*Fiesta del Maíz*). Focusing on corn as the primary sustenance of the land, he helped the community reflect on the many ways that corn was a gift in their lives. At the same time, Father Grande used the feast to consider the value of rural women as the perfect embodiment of the people.[46] The significance of this celebration was recalled by a former Delegate of the Word from Aguilares: "He invented [the celebration of] it. He said that we should give thanks to God for the fruits that we had sown and that we had gathered from the earth."[47] Quijano further described Father Rutilio's introduction of the festivity:

> That God is making the harvest abundant through the earth and the rain and your work. Let's have a party... First all those who have corn and corn fields. Bring in corn... And those with milk, give milk. Those who have sugar, they should give sugar, cinnamon. And bring what you can give because we are not going to sell the corn beverage (*atole*), we will give it to the people.[48]

In celebrating the beauty of corn, the parish members were being formed as a community of believers who gave attention to the significance of corn but also to valuing the women who contributed to the lifeblood of the people. At the heart of this feast was the centrality of God, or as a former student of Grande expressed:

> ... he had the capacity of taking the festivities or traditions that already existed and converting

> them into a true liturgical expression. Trying to find out what the true meaning was [of those celebrations]. What was the truth of those celebrations? And to bring them closer to the current history to see how that celebration helps in the present moment to a transformation of the situation in which we live.[49]

Grande's love for the popular religion of the people was evident to those who met him over the years. It was evident to the seminarians who noted his pride in being Salvadoran, in contrast to the predominantly Spanish clergy who resided in the seminary at the time. He gave the seminarians opportunities to participate in the patronal feasts, and to partake in the festivities that accompany these events. As a matter of fact, many of the seminarians came from these local communities. It was a way that Father Grande used to ensure that they would remain connected to their beginnings.

Aside from the popular faith expression of the people, Rutilio enjoyed serving as the master of ceremony for the diverse church religious events. He had a special love for the liturgy. As a young boy, he had been introduced to the liturgy by his devout grandmother who attended the town's church. As an ordained priest, Rutilio meticulously prepared and outlined every ritual in writing. Each step of the Mass followed clear instructions on how it was to be done, and by whom. Those who knew him well, or who worked with him, greatly understood that he would tolerate neither a lack of preparation of the liturgy nor any disregard for the sacred vessels. In essence, Grande gave attention to the liturgy because it led to union with God.[50]

He had a talent for linking prayer, popular expressions of faith, and liturgy to the contemporary world that Salvadorans were living. He saw salvation history in the context of the modern world, reinforcing the Gospel imperative that prayer and good works be united. As a matter of fact, his familiarity with the Constitution of the Republic of El Salvador was often connected to his sermons and Eucharistic celebration. As prefect of discipline in the minor seminary, and as one of the few Salvadorans on the seminary faculty, he was designated to teach a course on "Politi-

Memory and Legacy

cal Constitution" that focused on the country's Constitution. In teaching it, he became very familiar with the rights the Constitution promised to uphold for the Salvadoran people. In teaching the Political Constitution, Grande did not limit his teaching to the general concepts contained in the text, rather he made specific references and linked them to the current situation. In doing so, he demonstrated how, in many respects, the Constitution was not being upheld. He invited the students to be critical, and as far as possible, to find a way to improve that situation.[51] In his sermons, Grande would often refer to the Constitution of the Republic of El Salvador. On one occasion, referring to some law that had not been respected, he held up the Constitution waving it in his hand, and said: "Here is the Constitution that the President gave me, and here is his signature. But if it is not respected, and the laws are not carried out, what good is it?"[52] And, with that, as Father Grande held up the Constitution, he unintentionally flung it down the center aisle of the church.

Perhaps, one of his least known contributions is the method that Rutilio used in catechizing. Surprisingly for some, among his personal belongings, Father Grande left behind a hand-written manual of approximately seventy pages entitled *The Practice of Catechism*. A small book intended to be used in the formation of catechists, it was a supplement to an earlier document on Catechesis that he had written in July 1965. As was his custom, Grande meticulously laid out the process to be used in forming catechists. Rutilio Grande was a gifted teacher. He often turned to the scripture when he taught the people about God. As Eva Menjivar recalls:

> He was chosen because he was a very spirit-filled man. And so much so that he could put the Gospel in the hands of the people, with all simplicity. I remember when he explained the parable of the sower. He liked it because with the peasants they understood it wondrously, and so quickly... And one would be left admiring how he simplified the parable so that people could understand.[53]

And, many did leave understanding the parables so well that they became Delegates of the Word, and were able to celebrate the Word of God with others. And, they would themselves share Scripture reflections that were so profound as to come from the heart of God.[54] Some of these gifted teachers later became catechists. To Rutilio Grande's great sorrow, some of these catechists were the first ones to be assassinated. Grande, the master teacher, lived to see the outcome of how well his students had learned the message that he had passed onto them.[55]

Memory Celebrated in Song and Murals

Decades have passed since the death of the martyred Grande, but the memory of the man still lives on through the many contributions that he offered so generously during his lifetime to the Church, to the country of El Salvador, to his family and Jesuit community, and to all those he met and to whom he ministered. The memory of Rutilio Grande is also found in the songs sung in church or around a shared meal. The memory of Father Tilo, as he was affectionately known by some, is also painted on many walls throughout countless neighborhoods in El Salvador.

Father Rutilio Grande was murdered on 12 March 1977. News of his assassination struck a chord in the hearts of many Salvadorans. Upon hearing the news, the Catholic radio station, YSAX, transmitted the account of the murders of him and his companions: 72-year-old Manuel Solórzano and 15-year-old Nelson Rutilio Lemus. Grande's pastoral colleagues, friends, and Jesuit brothers took turns broadcasting the news.

Over the coming days, YSAX shared reflections on the events offering recollections of the much beloved Padre Tilo. Others took pen to paper and wrote songs marking the tragedy. On Monday, 14 March 1977, the funeral Mass for the three victims was celebrated in the cathedral. Afterwards, their bodies were taken to El Paisnal to be buried inside the town's church. After the services, as people were leaving the church a group of guitarists played several of the songs that had been spontaneously composed to honor Father Grande. Some of these songs were by anonymous composers, while others were written by well-known composers such as Jorge Palencia, Don José, and Piquín (Guillermo Cuéllar). March 12 was forever remembered in their lyrics. Songs written by a campesino of El Paisnal speaks to the death of Father Rutilio and of the cross that was placed alongside the road where he was killed.

Despite such profound sadness, the lyrics to these songs point to a death that promises light: "There where you fell, there we left your cross; But it's not just wood but it's also light. Already with this I say goodbye; May God hold them in his glory; This great murder will never be erased from history."[56] The solemnness of that day is underscored in these lyrics written by an anonymous composer:

> The news arrives that they have killed the man of my temple. He was killed by the cruel assassins, and also with him fell two campesino brothers. Father Tilo, you died with your people… Father Tilo, they destroyed your body, but your spirit will always live on in those who also follow your example.[57]

Four of the archival songs were written by Jorge Palencia. His lyrics speak of a persecuted people and of: "The prayer that sows in the furrow liberation… They struck out against your voice, campesino priest, many voices were silent, yours was not silent."[58] In "Bells for Grande" (*Campanas para Grande*) Palacios writes about the silenced bells that quietly watch the rich harvest of the land fertilized with Father Rutilio's blood. And, it sings: "Your voice throbs and resonates through the mountains and canals; It is the libertarian cry that makes the tyrant, the oppressor, the bloodthirsty tremble."[59]

In a couple of his songs, Palencia refers specifically to the death of Grande or to the aftermath of his assassination. In an alarming tone, his song "Aguilares Heroíco," describes the cruel days of military occupation in Aguilares that filled the town with terror and destruction. Despite this, the final stanza proclaims the people's determination to struggle for their liberation, and the enduring presence of the prophets: "The prophets will die, Aguilares won't be silenced even if death comes disguised as rifles and flags."[60]

Palencia's final song, "The Ballad to Father Grande" recounts the tragic events. It is among one of the most well-known in the country.

Rutilio Grande

> *On the 12 of March of 1977*
> *they killed Padre Grande*
> *on his way to El Paisnal.*
> *Traveling with Padre Tilo*
> *The humble campesinos*
> *Manuel and Rutilio Lemus*
> *on the way to preach the gospel.*
> *Father Grande would say,*
> *those who have more*
> *should share the land of the wealthy*
> *for the poor have paid the price.*[61]

In this song's final lines, the ballad speaks of God's justice and, although Father Grande was killed, he did not die. The campesinos that he lived and died for remember him—Chabela, Don Nicolás, Don Pedro, and all those who join the struggle in their fight for justice.

Similar themes are found in some of the songs composed by Piquín (Guillermo Cuéllar). The lyrics of several of his songs found in Grande's archives draw attention to the town of Aguilares after the death of Father Grande and his traveling companions, Manuel Solorzano and the young boy, Nelson Rutilio:

> *Death bruised your face—land of brave canals. Your name grows in strength Aguilares—with the blood of the dead. Your story flourished simply—a rhythm of hunger and patience and the flower of your courageous consciousness grew stronger than the sun itself.*[62]

In the end, it is the emerging voice of the prophet and the cry of human struggle, which will be listened to.[63] In "Sabes y Vos'os," Piquín points to what is known… those who govern the lands, that provoke wars and sow evil.[64]

But, of all the songs that he composed that somehow resurrected the presence and memory of Father Rutilio Grande, the most well-known is a song often used to bless a meal and gathering—"Let us go now to the Banquet." A banquet table that gathered all humankind and gave to each an equal share in the fruits of the earth:

Let us all go to the banquet, to the supper of creation, each with a stool of his own [to sit upon], each has a place and a mission... God invites all the poor to this common table made so by faith, where there are no borders and no one is missing what they need.[65]

A final song composed by an unnamed woman from the town of Cojutepeque brings to memory the unforgettable date of 12 March 1977, when Rutilio was killed along with a campesino and a young boy. She describes how they were traveling to the hometown of Father Grande to preach the Gospel, and God permitted his death so that in heaven Rutilio could raise his voice in song. Asking for the assassins to be forgiven, this composer ends: "And with this I say goodbye I say goodbye with great love, here I finish these lovely words with great sadness and sorrow."[66]

While sadness and sorrow were evident in the lyrics of the different songs composed to honor and remember the martyred pastor of Aguilares, his memory and voice are etched in the history of El Salvador. His name alone resurrects the memory of a man of humble roots who loved his people and believed in their right to the fruits of creation and to their dignity. The ballads and hymns have become part of the musical lexicon of the country, and are found in many hymnals.

The Murals

The memory of Rutilio Grande is not only carried in song. It is found painted in murals throughout countless neighborhoods in El Salvador. These murals keep him alive in the memory of those who knew and loved this good man. In the history of El Salvador, one of the often-depicted mural images is that of Rutilio Grande. The memory of Father Tilo, as he was lovingly called, is preserved in artwork boldly painted on the walls throughout the country's neighborhoods. Over the decades since his death, the presence of murals dedicated to the memory of Rutilio Grande have marked the entrance to El Paisnal, his hometown. These murals communicate the memories of how people of the town remember Father Tilo. Some of the murals have faded with time and a few have been painted over. However, copies and photos of these original murals have given them an ongoing presence.

One of the earliest murals is painted with the characteristically bright colors associated with the style of the small Salvadoran village of La Palma. It bore the title: "Father Tilo and Monseñor Romero: Prophets of Liberation" (*P. Tilo y Mons. Romero: Profetas de Liberación*). In the mural, both Rutilio Grande and Archbishop Romero are featured standing side-by-side. In the background is a painting of the small church of St. Joseph of El Paisnal, and in front of the two men, children extend their arms toward them or appear to encircle them. The mountains and volcanoes of the country can be seen in the foreground. On the right side of the murals, townspeople are depicted moving in a procession led by a man carrying a candle. They are flanked by tall, nutritious corn stalks. In the sky, balloons rise upwards toward a bright sun. On the far side of the painting, a basket is filled to the brim with bread and a jug can be seen. All of these signs were brought about by a true liberation.

In 2006, a mural project led by Isaías Mata and the Salvadoran association of art and culture workers known as ASTAC, created a mural entitled, "The Historical Memory of the Present" (*La Memoria Historica del Presente*). Locked arm-in-arm, a man holds a harvesting sickle while a woman has the Constitution of the Republic of El Salvador. On either side of them are men and women holding up their arms in the signature gesture of protest. They represent rural people who work the land in El Paisnal and surrounding towns.

These murals and many more continue to communicate Father Rutilio's love for the poor of his homeland. In El Salvador, the people have not forgotten how, in the midst of such violent and devastating realities, Jesuit Rutilio Grande gave them reason to hope, dream, and struggle for a better world. The vibrant communities that were formed during the three years of Rutilio's pastorship in Aguilares were many. Even today, the smiling image of Grande is the memory that continues to live in the hearts of many in El Salvador. The gifts he gave during his lifetime were a blessing then and now.

NOTES

1. Interview with Rutilio Sánchez, 1 July 2014. Spanish citation: "Si usted hablaba con el P. Rutilio Grande no descubría si había celebrado misa, si había hecho oración, o de donde venia. Siempre llegaba con aquella su sonrisa."
2. Ibid. Spanish citation: "El muy conservador, siempre muy puestecito… Siempre sonriente. Era una de las cualidades que tenia."
3. Ibid. Spanish citation: "Era un hombre de muy buenas relaciones con nosotros. No podemos acusarlo a consideración de otros de mal character. No. Lo podemos recordar como un sacerdote sonriente que permitía, y nos escuchaba, ¿verdad? Dialogante."
4. Interview with Manuel Quijano, 3 July 2014. Spanish citation: "Más de sacerdote, un padre humano, pues. Como de familia, un padre de familia…sincero par hablar, para tratarnos. El era totalmente abierto con todos, ¿verdad? Y eso de comer junto con nosotros. Llegaban los misioneros a los cantones a comer frijoles. Eso que teníamos nosotros, eso tenían que comer."
5. Ibid. Spanish citation: "No comían aparte, sino que junto con nosotros. ¿Cuando es que hemos visto un cura con nosotros en este estilo, que es bien placentero con toda la gente?"
6. Rutilio Sánchez: Spanish citation: "Porque él no era una persona recluida. Que el era aparentemente tímido, pienso yo. Tímido en el sentido que no es de esos espontáneos. Tenía esa suavidad que, se puede decir, a la timidez. No era un hombre esplendoroso, ¿verdad? Pero su sonrisa ganaba bastantes espacios…"
7. Interview with Miguel Ventura, 6 July 2014.
8. Ibid. Spanish citation: "…era una hombre dialogante, ese hombre abierto. Cuando había que exigir disciplina, exigía disciplina."
9. Ibid. Spanish citation: "El no regañaba. Él decía las cosas y decía: "Si tienes algo que decir, dilo o después.""
10. Ibid. Spanish citation: "Él decía una frase muy campesina: Aunque sea remendado, pero limpio." This phrase is often used by the poor who do not have much to wear. Consequently, they will often wear their best despite the fact that they have to mend or wash their dress item often. But, they do it in order to carry themselves in a dignified manner.
11. This description was shared by those who knew him. In their memory, he carried himself with quiet dignity. Grande was remembered by some as a soft-spoken, well-mannered, and handsome man.
12. Interview with Antonio Ocaña, 1 July 2014.
13. Ibid. Spanish citation: "…cuando empezaba una cosa, le gustaba paso a paso. No le gustaba el desorden. No le gustaba saltar etapas. Era parte de su carácter y de su manera de ser de el. Empezamos con esto, seguimos con esto, hasta llegar al final. …es que aprendí que aunque las cosas no se terminen. Porque no es el solo objetivo terminar, sino aprender hasta donde se puede llegar."
14. Ibid. Spanish citation: " …le gustaba discutir en la búsqueda, porque era un gran buscador."
15. Ibid. Spanish citation: "El fue, como quien dice, ese mediator bonito, simpático que defendía esas actitudes nuevas nuestras que para muchos pues iba a darles escándalo."
16. Ibid. Spanish citation: "Mire, monseñor, pues eso es lo más normal. Vivimos en otro tiempo."
17. Interview with Octavio Cruz, 15 November 2017. Spanish citation: "Porque era un hombre integro."
18. Interview with Manuel Quijano. Spanish citation: "Ustedes estan perdidas. Porque ustedes quieren quedar bien con Dios, pues están quedando mal con sus hermanos. Desde este momento les prohíbo que vengan a dejar flores aquí. Porque ese dinero que ustedes vienen y compran esas flores, no es lo que ustedes tienen. Es de lo que les roban a sus trabajadores y Dios no quiere eso."
19. Interview with Rutilio Sánchez, a former student of Grande's who shared: Spanish citation:

"Soportaba los malos chistes que le contábamos. No nos contaba chistes, pero no nos prohibía. Al contrario, siempre decía: "Oye, fulano, mira tienes algún chiste?"

20. Ibid. Spanish citation: "El era devoto del chilate, de todo lo típico, ¿verdad? Cuando habían fiestas en el seminario, le pedía a las religiosas que nos hacían la comida que nos dieran comidas típicas: chilate, pupusas, yuca. A diferencia, pues, de que cuando tuvimos tal vez alguna vez algunos otros nos daban sándwich, nos daban pastel, verdad?"
21. Rodolfo Cardenal, *Historia de una Esperanza, Vida de Rutilio Grande*, El Salvador: UCA Editores, 1992, 54.
22. Interview with Octavio Cruz, 12 May 2014. Spanish citation:" ...yo no pude percibir algo como eso, sino que yo más bien lo que veía era como, como la lucha interna de cualquiera por tratar de ser fiel...sentí que era como el testimonio de una persona que esta queriendo ser fiel a su carisma y a lo que Dios le esta pidiendo. Pueda ser que los que lo conocieron si tuvo algún problema de ese tipo y que haya necesitado tratamiento o cualquier cosa."
23. Ibid. Spanish citation: "...era más bien equilibrado. Sólo cuando lé se ponía mal, podemos decir, cuando no hacía la siesta."
24. Ibid. Spanish citation: "Porque el tenía la costumbre de que, aunque sean 10 minutos, decía el "porque si no, paso mala tarde."
25. Interview with Salvador Carranza, S.J., 6 May 2014. Spanish citation: "Various problemas tuvo siempre. A la hora de hablar externamente, no. Se transformaba y se ponía en el lugar de esos que estaba hablando...y para nada le salía la duda. Eso era dudar. ¿Ésto o ésto? Era muy, muy, muy de él. Andar con dudas, consultaba muchísimo. De Aguilares venia a hablar con los maestros de la UCA muy frecuentemente sobre esto que están haciendo los campesinos, tomar por aquí esto, o insister en esto."
26. Rutilio Grande archive, Datos Biograficos del P. Rutilio Grande Garcia, S.J.. Spanish citation: "A los comienzos de su vida religiosa manifestó una clara debilidad nerviosa...Tenía depresiones sicológicas y se temio por su salud mental. ..fue consciente de esa limitacion, sufrio por ello, pero no se dejo llevar de ella; la acepto, trabajo por dominarla y la supero. Tal vez por esta enfermedad sus cualidades naturales no brillaron tanto; tal vez esta enfermedad fue el motivo por el que Rutilio domino mejor sus arrebatos, sus impulsos y se pusiera con mas seguridad y sencillez en las manos de Dios."
27. Interview with Octavio Cruz. Spanish citation: "...con más razón la obra de Dios se manifestó de una mejor manera en él. Porque a pesar de las limitaciones, él pudo cumplir con la misión, y él pudo responder a lo que el Señor le pedía."
28. Ibid. Spanish citation: "...ahí en la parroquia de Aguilares pude yo, pues, experimentar esta dimensión que le decía de cómo Rutilio se transformaba. Uno era el Rutilio cuando estábamos platicando en las reunions, al Rutilio que cuando estaba en la homilia era un hombre lleno de Dios, con una fortaleza, con una capacidad de comunicarse y darse a entender de las personas, con un lenguaje sencillo, un lenguaje popular, pero también con una gran valentía para denunciar el pecado y las injusticias."
29. Interview with Octavio Cruz. Spanish citation: "... es cierto se había formado antes del Concilio Vaticano, pero él pues tuvo una mente abierta al Concilio II...Ese Dios de la Biblia al Dios que da la respuesta a la problemática humana, pues con ese Dios nos encontrabamos en los sacramentos."
30. Interview with Miguel Ventura. Spanish citation: "De tal manera que esta formación nos va a llevar a nosotros todos los seminaristas a un abrir las puertas del seminario. El seminario era bastante cerrado con aquella concepción de Trento, ¿verdad? Hay que formar a los sacerdotes, pues, en un ambiente, voy a decir, doctrinal, eclesial muy encerrado, sumamente encerrado. Para la concepción de Rutilio Grande es: no puede haber evangelización salvífica liberadora si es que el futuro sacerdote no entra en contacto con la realidad. Entonces, Rutilio Grande creo que es el que abre también puertas, ya en los años más avanzados, a que tengamos nosotros en la planificación pastoral análisis de la realidad del país. Análisis de la realidad eclesial. Análisis, si quieres, de la realidad latinoamericana. ¿Pero todo y para qué? Para que esa evangelización tenga un marco, un marco transformador de la realidad."

31. Many of Rutilio Grande's seminarians and pastoral ministers shared the same appreciation for the innovative pastoral approach that he created for the students. Miguel Ventura, Rutilio Sánchez, Octavio Cruz, Benito Tovar, Gregorio Landaverde, Eva del Carmen Menjivar.
32. Interview with Rutilio Sánchez. Spanish citation: "Fui encargado de planificación. Por supuesto, junto con el. Me tocaba recoger todas las experiencias cotidianas, ordenarlas, sistematizarlas. Y, junto con un equipo que habíamos formado de los mismos compañeros, sacabamos conclusiones. Eso fue importante para mi. Fue una experiencia muy bonita porque me ayudó a descubrir algunas posibilidades que uno tiene en la organización."
33. Octavio Cruz: Spanish citation: "Esto esta bueno, pero vos tenés mas capacidad. Por eso te pongo 7. No Porque fuera malo, sino porque dijo "tú puedes más." Y yo recuerdo que no me molesté, sino que me sentí retado y apreciado. Porque sabia que él me apreciaba. O sea, tenía como mucha confianza y esperanza en mi de que yo tenía que ser un buen sacerdote."
34. Interview with Salvador Carranza, 6 May 2014. Spanish citation: "Ahí Rutilio se distinguió muchísimo. El seminario, pues,pone el Concilio Vaticano II, y con los que venían nuevos, con Rutilio e incluso con otros profesores nuevos, pues: "hay que cambiar esto o hay que ponerlo al día." En esa línea estaba muy Rutilio. Los seminaristas también hay que crear en ellos un sacerdote para el día de hoy y de acuerdo al Concilio y a la Conferencia Episcopal famosa de Medellín."
35. Interview with Miguel Ventura, 6 July 2014. Spanish citation: "…si hay un hombre clave en la formación de ese nuevo clero, porque después hay que ver los frutos, los resultados, toda esa generación de héroes, de sacerdotes mártires, fueron los que convivieron con él en la formación. Un Octavio Ortiz, un Neto Barrera, un Alfonso Navarro, ¿verdad? Este… Manuel Reyes, que también es de esta generación. Abrego, Ernesto Abrego. Bueno, todos esos sacerdotes diocesanos hay que ubicarlos dentro de los años."
36. In an interview (21 July 2015) with Father Benito Tovar, he indicated that pastoral attention was already being given to campesinos communities by diocesan priests prior to Rutilio Grande's pastoral work in Aguilares. While this may be true, nevertheless, there was something in the method and approach that Grande used that seemed to make a unique contribution to ministry at the time.
37. Ibid. Spanish citation: "Pero el hombre estaba encima. Estaba como conduciendo todo este proceso. Esto estaba echando las bases de una nueva visión, de una fe liberadora. No podemos nosotros tener una salvación en la historia, o construir una historia de la salvación si no entramos contacto con la realidad. Y eso fue lo que formó, en gran medida, en nuestro talante, en nuestro carácter, en nuestra visión, ¿verdad? De cómo llegar a construir en El Salvador una Iglesia del pueblo. Porque iba también construyéndose esa Iglesia del pueblo, pero haciendo que los sujetos de nuestro pueblo impulsaran también, a la luz de la fe, los cambios."
38. Interview with Eva del Carmen Menjivar, 7 May 2018. Spanish citation: " Yo pienso que el P. Grande fue un hombre muy iluminado por Dios. Con todo el Espíritu se puede decir, de Jesús. Que revolucionó toda ese caminar de las comunidades. Allí se crearon comunidades en todos los cantones…"
39. Ibid. Spanish citation: "Ahora, ya no vamos a hacer, ya no vamos a esperar que vengan misioneros de afuera, ¿verdad? Sino que los misioneros tenemos que ser nosotros mismos."
40. Interview with Manuel Quijano, 3 July 2014. Spanish citation: "Yo no había ido a la escuela. No podía reconocer la abecedaria. De ahí no podia nada, leer nada. Pero, dije yo, primero Dios, si vienen aquí a Potrero Grande, dije yo, debo de ver como consigo una bibia. Y deletreado, tengo que aprender a leer, y voy a aprender. Me "bendicio" Dios porque cuando llegaron allá, fui el primerito al que dieron un libro."
41. Interview with Eva del Carmen Menjivar, 7 May 2018. Spanish citation: "Era un hombre muy sencillo, muy sensato, muy humilde. El iba tomando de las cosas…Por ejemplo, en el campo, les decía a los campesinos: "Vamos a estudiar ahora el gran capitulo. Lo vamos a pensar que el capitulo grande es toda una hacienda—como sabía que la mayoría de la gente trabajaba en haciendas—y que los versículos son los hectares o los pedacitos de terreno que les toca trabajar a ustedes."

Rutilio Grande

42. Interview with Manuel Quijano, 3 July 2014. Spanish citation: "Léanlo despacio, vayan interpretando. No solo lean por quererlo leer. Mastiquen lo que leen. Piensen y hablen lo que ustedes piensen. Porque solo así ustedes van a conocer a Cristo, y Cristo los va a conocer a ustedes. Ustedes van a ser servidores de Cristo. De otro no van a ser servidor. Mios no van a ser. Son de Cristo. Pero ustedes tienen que estar, "dijo," preparados. Y esta es nuestra mision."
43. Ibid. Manuel Quijano recalled the conversations that the people of Aguilares had with their pastor, Rutilio Grande, as they became more aware of the injustice of their working and living situation. He shared this in an interview on 3 July 2014. Spanish citation: "Bueno, nosotros lo que queremos es organizarnos como campesinos. Porque si no nos organizamos no tenemos derecho de pedir lo que nosotros necesitamos y que el mismo Evangelio nos esta exigiendo que tenemos que exigir justicia. Lo que estamos viviendo es una injusticia."
44. Ibid. Spanish citation: "…por mi causa ustedes van a sufrir, a ustedes los van a perseguir, a ustedes los van a "carcelar," los van a garrotear, los van a expulsar de sus comunidades, y los van hasta a matar, pero no se aflijan. Porque Jesucristo mismo dice, "que el que da la vida por su pueblo y por el Evangelio, tiene vida eternal. ¿Que mas quieren ustedes?
45. An insight shared with me by Octavio Cruz, 12 May 2014.
46. See: *Romero & Grande: Companions on the Journey*, 77, for an expanded explanation.
47. Interview with Manuel Quijano, 3 July 2014. Spanish citation: "El lo invento. Que decía que había que darle gracias a Dios por los frutos que habíamos sembrado y que habíamos recogido de la tierra."
48. Ibid. Spanish citation: "Eso Dios," dijo, "se los esta multiplicando a ustedes a través de la tierra y de la lluvia y del trabajo de ustedes. Hagamos una fiesta," dijo. "Una vez todos los que tengan maíz, milpas, y elote. Tráiganlo el elote, dijo. Y los que tengan leche, den leche. Los que tienen azúcar, que den azucar, canela. Y traigan lo que puedan dar porque el atole no lo vamos a vender, lo vamos a regalar.
49. Interview with Octavio Cruz, 12 May 2014.
50. Cf. *Romero & Grande*, 79.
51. A memory shared by Octavio Cruz, a former seminarian of Rutilio Grande, 12 May 2014. I have paraphrased his words for greater clarity. Spanish citation: "…al estudiar la Constitución Política no se limitaba unicamente a lo conceptual del texto, sino que él hacía una referencia a la realidad con el texto, mostrando como en muchos aspectos, en ese tiempo, pues no se respetaba la Constitución. Y nos invitaba a que nosotros deberíamos también ser críticos y, en la medida de lo posible, pues buscar la manera de cómo mejorar esa situación."
52. Recalled by Octavio Cruz who witnessed this moment while Father Grande was giving a sermon in the church of Our Lord of Mercies in Aguilares. Spanish citation: "Y aquí está Constitución que el señor president me regaló, aquí esta la firma que él puso. Pero si no se respeta, sino se cumplen las leyes, ¿de qué sirve? Y ¡pum! La aventó. Y se fue así en el centro de la nave de la iglesia y todo mundo así. Alguien se levantó, la fue a tomar de nuevo.
53. Interview with Eva del Carmen Menjivar, 7 May 2014. Spanish citation: "Lo escogieron porque era un hombre muy lleno de Espíritu. Y tanto así que podía poner al Evangelio tan en las manos del pueblo, con toda la sencillez. Yo recuerdo cuando explicaba esta parábola del sembrador. Le gustaba porque con los campesinos eso lo entendían a mil maravillas, pero así,…Y uno quedaba admirado como el se bajaba tanto para que la gente entendiera."
54. Paraphrasing of a memory shared by Eva del Carmen Menjivar, 7 May 2014.
55. Ibid.
56. The Jesuit archives included copies of songs composed upon the death of Rutilio Grande. This one is written by an anonymous composer self-described as a "campesino" from El Paisnal, Grande's hometown. Spanish citation: "Ahí donde tú caiste, ahí dejamos tu cruz; pero no es sólo madera sino que también es luz. Ya con ésta me despido; que Dios los tenga en la Gloria; este gran asesinato jamás lo borrará la historia." (Archivo de la Provincial Centroamericana de la Compañía de Jesús [Archive of the Centroamerican Province of the Society of Jesus], San Salvador, El Salvador)

57. Ibid. Spanish citation: "Padre Tilo has muerto con tu gente... Padre Tilo, acabaron con tu cuerpo, pero tu espíritu siempre vive en aquél que tambien sigue tu ejemplo."
58. "Al Cura Campesino', song written by Jorge Palencia. Spanish citation: "...la oración que siembra en el surco liberación. Apuñalaron tu voz, cura campesinos muchas voces callaron, la tuya no calló."
59. "Campanas para Grande," song written by Jorge Palencia. Spanish citation: "tu voz palpita y resuena por los montes y cañales; es el grito libertario que hace temblar al tirano, al opresor, al sanguinario."
60. "Aguilares Heroíco," song written by Jorge Palencia. Spanish citation: "Los profetas morirán, Aguilares no callará aunque se disfrace la muerte de fúsil y de banderas."
61. "Corrido al P. Grande," song written by Jorge Palencia. Spanish citation: "El día 12 de marzo del año 77' mataron al Padre Grande, iba camino a El Paisnal. Iba con el Padre Tilo los humildes campesiños Manuel y Rutilio Lemus a predicar el evangelio. El Padre Grande decía quien tenga mas que reparta la tierra de los ricos, es porque al pobre le cuesta."
62. "Aguilares," written by songwriter Guillermo Cuéllar, known as Piquín. Spanish citation: "Pateó la muerte tu rostro--tierra de bravos cañales tu nombre crece Aguilares--con la sangre de los muertos. Tu historia brotó sencilla--a ritmo de hambre y paciencia y la flor de tu consciencia valiente crecía ganándole al sol."
63. Ibid. Spanish citation: "...será la voz del profeta y el grito de guerra lo que han de escuchar."
64. "Sabes y Vos'os," written by Piquín. Spanish citation: "Sabes, quien gobierna estas tierras, quien provoca las guerras, quienes siembran maldad."
65. Song written by Piquín. Spanish citation: "Vamos todos al banquete, a la cena de la creación, cada cual, con su taburete, tiene un puesto y una mission. Dios invita a todos los pobres a esta mesa común por la fe, donde no hay acaparadores y a nadie le falta el con qué."
66. Song attributed to a woman from Cojetepeque. Spanish citation: "Ya con esta me despido yo me despido con grande amor, aquí termino estas lindas palabras con gran tristeza y grande dolor."

APPENDIX

MARCH 1977 PHOTOGRAPHS

Photographs are courtesy of the Archbishop Romero Center at the University of Central America in San Salvador, which is also the source for the descriptive information in the captions.

This page shows the bullet-ridden vehicle in which Fr. Grande and two companions were ambushed and murdered on 12 March 1977 while travelling from Aguilares to El Paisnal.

Following pages show scenes from Blessed Rutilio Grande's funeral; his domicile at the convent at Aguilares; and scenes of the massive crowds at the Eucharistic concelebration, 20 March 1977, at the Metropolitan Cathedral of the Holy Savior in San Salvador. This Mass, the Sunday following the murder and burial of Fr. Grande and his two companions, was planned by Archbishop Romero and the Salvadoran bishops as a memorial to the three slain men.

Front and rear views of the death car in which Fr. Rutilio Grande, S.J., Manuel Solórzano and Nelson Rutilio Lemus were ambushed and murdered while travelling to El Paisnal around 6:00 p.m. on 12 March 1977.

Rutilio Grande

Exterior and interior perspectives of the funeral Mass on 14 March 1977 in San Salvador, including the massive crowds in the plaza, and Blessed Rutilio Grande's casket.

March 1977 Photographs

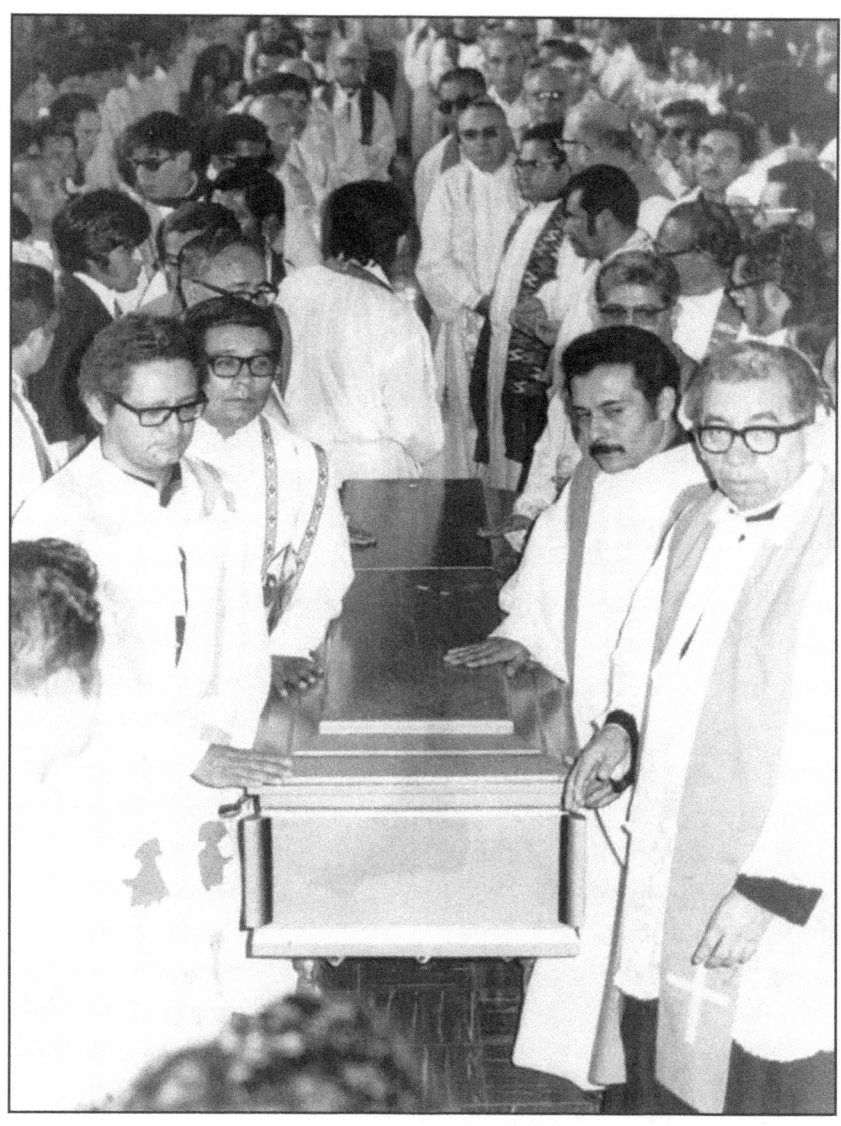

Rutilio Grande

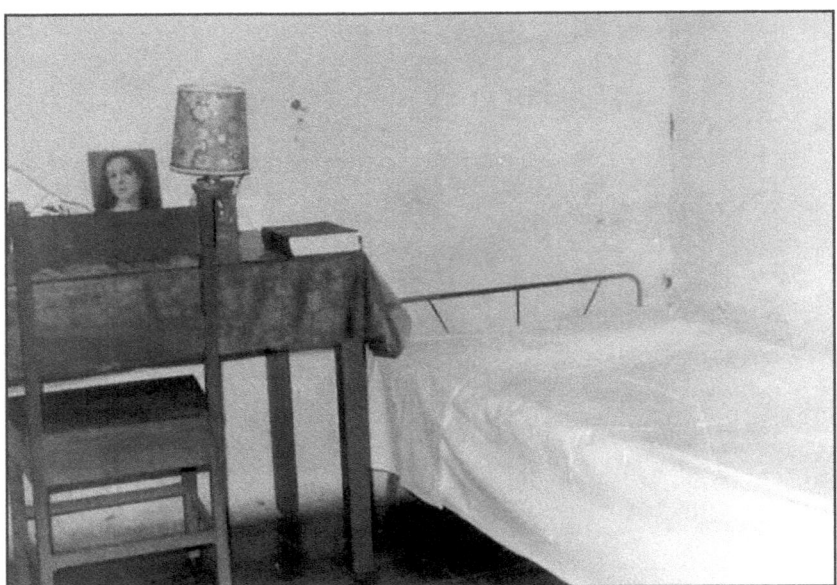

Fr. Grande's domicile in Aguilares. Views include exterior veranda (top), corner of his room showing his bed and writing table (lower), and a resource library corner including a perspective of the height of his room (opposite).

March 1977 Photographs

Rutilio Grande

Crowds gathered at the Eucharist celebrated at the doors of the Metrpolitan Cathedral in San Salvador, 20 March 1977. A small part of the massive crowd is pictured while gathered in the plaza (above). The people in front of the cathedral were packed densely (top, opposite). The altar is shown from above, flanked by many scores of priests as they concelebrated on this Feast of St. Joseph, the patron saint of El Paisnal (lower, opposite).

March 1977 Photographs

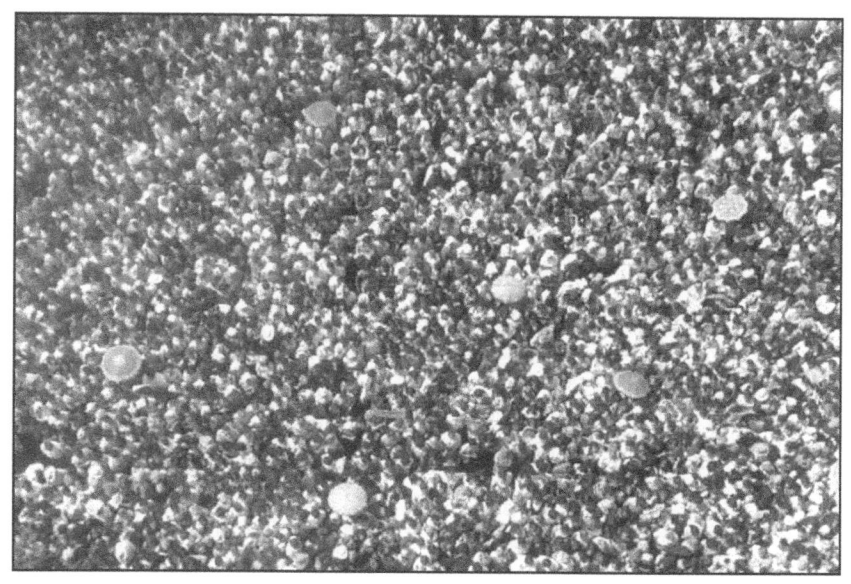

You may also enjoy an another book by Ana María Pineda

Romero and Grande: Companions On the Journey

Just three years after Rutilio Grande, SJ, was assassinated, Archbishop Óscar Romero was murdered while presiding at Mass for actively denouncing violations of the human rights of the most vulnerable people and defending the principles of protecting lives, promoting human dignity and opposing all forms of violence. Romero was canonized by Pope Francis as a saint on 14 October 2018.

Up to now, the stories about these men had grown elusive and vague, but Salvadoran native and Sister of Mercy Ana María Pineda has catapulted both these two martyrs into our collective consciences with accounts that are significantly personal and painstakingly researched during multiple trips to her homeland.

Archbishop Vincenzo Paglia, postulator for the cause of canonization of Óscar Romero commented:
"It is impossible to know Romero without knowing Rutilio Grande."

"Understanding more fully their relationship is the special strength and contribution of the book Romero & Grande: Companions on the Journey. I recommend this book as an essential part of the living tradition of prophetic leadership in the Latin American Church."
– Robert S. Pelton, CSC, University of Notre Dame

Available directly from the publisher +1 772-932-7969
https://www.lectiopublishing.com/books.php?b=9

CPSIA information can be obtained
at www.ICGtesting.com
Printed in the USA
BVHW091746150222
629082BV00004B/255